Ceremony &
Celebration
Coronation Day
1953

# Ceremony & Celebration

# Coronation Day 1953

CHRISTOPHER LLOYD

WITH AN ESSAY BY
HUGH ROBERTS

What is the finest sight in the world? A Coronation.
What do people talk most about? A Coronation.
What is delightful to have passed? A Coronation.

Horace Walpole in a letter to Sir Horace Mann, written on
28 September 1761 following the coronation of George III

THE ROYAL COLLECTION

This publication has been
supported by KPMG.

Published by
Royal Collection Enterprises Ltd
St James's Palace, London SW1A 1JR

For a complete catalogue of current publications,
please write to the address above, or visit our website
on www.royal.gov.uk

ISBN 1 902163 65 6

British Library Cataloguing in Publication Data:
A catalogue record for this book is available from
the British Library.

Designed by LewisHallam
Produced by Book Production Consultants plc, Cambridge
Printed and bound by Graphicom, Italy

# Contents

The Crowning, from *Country Life*
*Picture Book of the Coronation*, 2 June 1953, No. 36.

# Acknowledgements

I am particularly grateful to Feliks Topolski's family, and especially the artist's children, Daniel and Teresa, for their enthusiastic support of *Ceremony and Celebration: Coronation Day 1953*, and for detailed information about their father's life. Visits to the studio and to *Memoir of the Century* under Hungerford Bridge were an integral part of understanding and interpreting the depiction of the *Coronation of Queen Elizabeth II* in Buckingham Palace.

Marcus Harrison and James Woodford, who knew Feliks Topolski, have also assisted.

In addition, I am indebted to Larry and Jill Carver who helped in elucidating various points about the artist's life and in gathering information about the present whereabouts of his works.

The assistance of Garter Principal King of Arms, Peter Gwynn-Jones, during a visit to see the papers relating to the Coronation at The College of Arms was both instructive and memorable.

I have been helped at every stage by Janice Sacher, who while working for the Royal Collection as a volunteer has devoted a great deal of time and energy to this project. The zestful way in which she threw herself into both the research and preparation of this book would undoubtedly have impressed even Feliks Topolski himself. Her challenges included searching for The Queen's Beasts, rediscovering the original recipe for Coronation Chicken, and total immersion in the twelve-hour BBC television coverage of Coronation Day.

Both the designer of this publication, Philip Lewis, and of the related exhibition in Buckingham Palace, George Carter, have been sympathetic to my feelings of nostalgia for the 1950s, extending from early televisions and refrigerators to Coronation souvenir books and Sir Norman Hartnell's dress designs.

CL

# The Coronation: history and meaning

THROUGHOUT BRITISH HISTORY the crowning of the sovereign has been a moment of the greatest significance. The celebrations have always been widespread and prolonged, uniting the nation in an outpouring of rejoicing, which in its expression of continuity at once acknowledges the potency of the past and gives rise to hope for the future. Official records, newspaper reports, personal memoirs and a multitude of images testify the degree to which coronation days have absorbed the attention of the whole nation. The mobilisation of resources, arranged by the Earl Marshal through The College of Arms, is a prodigious feat involving the various echelons of church and state, as well as a full supporting cast including composers, poets and (until 1831) herbstrewers (fig 1).

It is given to relatively few people to witness more than one coronation and so the uniqueness of the occasion is heightened for both the active participants and the observers. The naval administrator and diarist Samuel Pepys (1633–1703), who witnessed the English coronation of Charles II in 1661, wrote on 23 April, 'Now after all this, I can say that besides the pleasure of the sight of these glorious things, I may now shut my eyes against any other objects … as being sure never to see the like again in this world.' Some, however, did experience more than one coronation. Pepys's fellow diarist John Evelyn (1620–1706) attended three – those of Charles II, James II (1685) and William III and Mary II (1689) – with varying degrees of enthusiasm, but always with an eye to procedural differences. In the twentieth

century, the politician Sir Henry Channon (1897–1958) left scintillating accounts of the coronations of King George VI (1937) and Queen Elizabeth II (1953) in which he is both overawed by the ceremonial and appreciative of the party atmosphere.

All accounts of coronations, whether spontaneous or not, provide evidence of the significance of royal ceremonial. In earlier centuries, first-hand knowledge of such events was limited to those who attended them. Consequently, until the advent of the modern media, coronations (like all royal ceremonial) were, as the historian David Cannadine wrote in 1983, 'not so much shared, corporate events as remote, inaccessible group rites, performed for the benefit of the few rather than the edification of the many'. This by no means diminished the meaning or significance of the event; rather, it heightened the mystique because of its exclusivity. In modern times, the coronation has become more of a shared experience. In 1953 its political meaning remained the same, but the social context widened so that the celebrations were more of a collective event. The leading article in *The Times* for Coronation Day in 1953 stated that The Queen 'represents the life of her people … as men and women, and not in their limited capacity as Lords and Commons and electors. It is the glory of the social monarchy that it sets the human above the institutional.' Translated into other, more academic terms, an analysis of the Coronation of 1953 written by two sociologists, Edward Shils and Michael Young, referred to it as a 'national communion'

Fig. 1 'The King's Herbwoman (Miss Fellowes) with her six Maids, strewing the way with herbs', plate 5 from Sir George Nayler's *The Coronation of His Most Sacred Majesty King George the Fourth*, published in London by Henry George Bohn, 1837
Aquatint, 25.1 × 49 cm (9⅞ × 19¼")
Royal Collection (RCIN 1051582)

Traditionally the royal herbwoman and her six assistants scattered herbs and flowers in the path of the procession from Westminster Hall to the Abbey and back again (see fig. 11). The ceremony of strewing was related to the medieval idea of warding off evil smells and the plague. By the time of the Coronation of 1953 the herbwoman's role was symbolised by the bouquet of white flowers (orchids, lily of the valley, stephanotis and carnations; see fig. 75) presented by the Worshipful Company of Gardeners and carried by The Queen in the procession to the Abbey.

affirming 'the moral values by which the society lives'. Whatever interpretation is put on the ceremonial or the celebrations by historians, the primary purpose of the coronation is incontestable and has remained the same through the centuries.

The crowning of the sovereign is the declaration of secular authority within a specific religious context, according to established tradition. The church service itself retains aspects of secular procedure, but these are couched within religious terms of reference. Thus, while the central moment of the ceremony is the actual Crowning, the most reverent is the Anointing which sets the sovereign apart and indicates the divine origin of regal authority. As Walter Bagehot said in *The English Constitution* (1867):

> The English Monarchy strengthens our government with the strength of religion. It is commonly hidden like a mystery, and sometimes paraded like a pageant, but in neither case is it contentious.

The coronation, therefore, is an expression of the unity of church and state conjoined symbolically in a single person. Combining religious solemnity with carefully orchestrated pageantry, nearly every moment of the coronation ceremony is based on precedent. The form of service has evolved slowly over a period of a thousand years. The few innovations and shifts in emphasis that have occurred have done so as a result of changing historical circumstances. The establishment of the Church of England in 1536, when Henry VIII denied the authority of the papacy in Rome, was one such defining moment of immense significance.

The origins of the crowning and enthronement of a ruler are pre-Christian. Whether rulers in ancient societies were elected or hereditary, the validation of their status gave rise to the ritual of ceremonial. This involved identification by public acclamation; elevation either by being held aloft on a shield or in some other way enthroned; and the wearing of primitive forms of regalia.

By the time of the Roman Empire such ceremonial had begun to be codified, but with the Roman Emperor Constantine's conversion to Christianity in AD 312 and the division of the Empire into east and west the coronation began to take on a recognisably modern form. Constantine (r.306–337) symbolically united in himself the concept of empire and the idea of a Christian church. Consequently, the nature of the imperial office changed so that in effect the holder was not only the supreme ruler in a secular sense, but also the defender of the official religion of the Empire. The historical consequences of this development were enormous and in later centuries were to create tensions between church and state. The shift in power within the Roman Empire between the east (Constantinople) and the west (Rome), which began under Constantine, gave greater impetus to the redefinition of the ideology of imperial rule. Religious texts – predominantly from the Old Testament – were cited in support of the ruler's combined role defending both physical and spiritual boundaries. In essence, by

Fig. 2 *Life of St Edmund, King of East Anglia, c.1130*
Manuscript illumination, 27.4 × 18.7 cm (10¾ × 7¼")
New York, Pierpont Morgan Library (MS M.736, fol.22v.)

Edmund the Martyr (c.840–69) was the last of the Saxon kings of England. On refusing to share power with the Danish invaders he was tied to a tree and shot with arrows until his body was 'like a thistle covered with prickles'. His cult was established almost immediately and his body was eventually enshrined at the Abbey of Bury St Edmunds in Suffolk, which was founded in 1020. This *Life of St Edmund* was written and illuminated at the Abbey. The representation of the coronation is related to the Ottonian tradition in Germany.

the end of the fifth century the concept of imperial rule had been transmuted into the idea of a Christian empire where biblical prototypes were used not just to define leadership, but also to emphasise the divine source of power. On this basis coronations of extraordinary significance in European countries began to occur. The coronation of Charlemagne, King of the Franks, as Emperor by Pope Leo III in Rome on Christmas Day AD 800, for instance, was one of the most momentous occasions in European history for the future development of relations between church and state. Charlemagne (r.800–814) was in fact, if not in name, the first Holy Roman Emperor, combining military powers and cultural aspirations.

The standardisation of the coronation in England began with the Anglo-Saxon and Danish kings during the eighth and ninth centuries, when the hereditary principle of succession was becoming established (fig. 2). It is from this time that the first detailed description of a coronation survives – namely that of Edgar by Dunstan, Archbishop of Canterbury, in AD 973 at Kingston upon Thames in Surrey. The source is the biography of St Oswald, Archbishop of York, who assisted Dunstan. Much of the ceremonial was based on that which had evolved in Scandinavia, Germany, France, Spain and Italy and through this a consensus on what comprised a formal coronation was reached, although with different emphases according to country.

One of Edgar's successors, Edward the Confessor (r.1042–66), has a significant role in the history of the coronation, not as a result of his actions, but because of his reputation, leading to his canonisation in 1161. Although crowned at Winchester, Edward the Confessor is most closely associated with Westminster Abbey where he was buried. During the twelfth century the Abbey authorities declared that the royal regalia in their possession was that commissioned or even used by Edward the Confessor. This set of coronation regalia apparently comprised a crown, sceptre and orb, chalice and paten, as well as vestments. The crown, in particular, was encrusted with precious jewels and the vestments made of the richest materials. Whatever truth there was in the Abbey's claim, the regalia itself constituted the oldest surviving set in Europe. Furthermore, the fact that it was deposited in the Abbey gave the regalia greater prestige or sanctity than any of the items retained by an individual monarch for personal use.

The implication was that Edward the Confessor's regalia should be regarded as being of official status, for use by all subsequent monarchs. As such, it was added to, or adjusted, in accordance with the wishes of individual sovereigns and in some instances for their consorts. Around it the Abbey established a treasury which included a quantity of liturgical plate. The symbolic potency of the royal regalia is underlined by the description of it by Peter Heylyn, chaplain to Charles I (r.1625–49) and Prebendary of Westminster Abbey, who refers to it as kept 'in a secret place . . . not easily accessible to any, but such as know the mystery

Fig. 4 Wenceslaus Hollar (1607–77)
*The Coronation of Charles II*, 1661
Etching, 36.1 × 47.3 cm
(14¼ × 18¾")
Royal Collection (RCIN 750142)

This print gives a clear indication of the importance of the 'theatre' which was the space created in the crossing of Westminster Abbey where the principal moments in the ceremony were enacted. The view is towards the high altar and the King is shown twice, once on the dais in the Chair of State and again nearer the altar, seated in St Edward's Chair, being crowned by the Archbishop of Canterbury. The banks of seating in the north and south transepts were temporary.

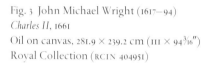

Fig. 3 John Michael Wright (1617–94)
*Charles II*, 1661
Oil on canvas, 281.9 × 239.2 cm (111 × 94³⁄₁₆")
Royal Collection (RCIN 404951)

This important state portrait was painted at the time of the Restoration. The emphasis on the new set of regalia underscores the authority of the monarch who is seated under a canopy embroidered with the royal coat of arms. Behind the canopy, seen to left and right, is a tapestry representing the Judgement of Solomon.

of it: never brought forth but at the Coronation of a King, or his going to Parliament'. After the execution of Charles I the regalia was either sold off or melted down and only the anointing spoon and three swords (those called Temporal Justice, Spiritual Justice and Mercy) survived. As a result, on his Restoration in 1660 Charles II commissioned from the royal goldsmith, Robert Vyner, a new set of regalia for his coronation, at a cost of £12,050 3s 5d (fig. 3). This is the regalia forming part of the Crown Jewels now displayed in the Jewel House in the Tower of London.

The association of Edward the Confessor with Westminster Abbey may have been influential in William the Conqueror's decision to be crowned there in 1066. This established a precedent and English coronations thereafter have customarily taken place at Westminster Abbey, just as coronation churches were identified at Reims in France and Aachen in Germany. Previous locations in England, such as Winchester,

Oxford, Kingston upon Thames, Gloucester, Canterbury and Bath, had been chosen more for convenience. The primacy of Westminster Abbey was confirmed in the thirteenth century during the reign of Henry III (1216–72), who felt a special veneration for Edward the Confessor. Taking his lead from France, specifically from Reims, he made substantial architectural additions to the Abbey. The east end was extended to create St Edward's Chapel with an elaborate shrine to the saint (1269) and emphasis was given to the crossing, where space was reserved for performing the coronation. This space was actually termed the 'theatre' and by moving the choir lower down the nave it allowed the various phases of the ritual to be enacted by the main participants with a clear view of the high altar (fig. 4). The triforium extending on all sides of the crossing afforded a spectacular viewing point for spectators and may have been designed with this purpose in mind.

Once Westminster Abbey had been acknowledged as the coronation church the service itself began to be refined. Accordingly, the fourteenth and fifteenth centuries witnessed both the climax of the medieval coronation and its development in a more modern form. A focus was provided by Edward I (r.1272–1307) who commissioned the Coronation Chair. Made of wood, it was raised first on a gilded step and then in the sixteenth century altered to rest on the backs of four gilded lions. Immediately below the seat was an opening for the stone of Scone, a symbol of royalty captured from the Scots in 1296. The presumed intention was to subjugate the Scots by transferring the stone to London. (The stone was returned to Scotland seven hundred years later in 1997, but will continue to be used at future coronation services.) Confusingly, the Coronation Chair came to be called St Edward's Chair, as though originating with Edward the Confessor.

Two manuscripts – both in the possession of Westminster Abbey – codified the ceremonial and the ritual of the coronation, in addition to identifying the main participants, and thus became points of reference for all subsequent coronations. The manuscripts are the *Westminster Missal* (c.1383–4) and the *Liber Regalis* (c.1390); both are lavishly illuminated. These sources not only provide details of the order of service and the numerous processions, but also clearly annex the coronation for the Abbey itself. These two manuscripts and others (fig. 5) reflect the outward magnificence

Fig. 5  *Apocalypse and Coronation (Ordo?) of Edward II or Edward III*, c.1320–30
Manuscript illumination, 37.5 × 25.4 cm (14¾ × 10″)
Cambridge, Corpus Christi College (MS 20, fol. 68r)

The bulk of this manuscript illustrates the Apocalypse, but it is completed by an account of the coronation service for either Edward II (r. 1307–27) or Edward III (r. 1327–77). The book was commissioned by Henry de Cobham who could have participated in either event. The king is shown surrounded by ecclesiastics and nobility.

and intense religiosity of the coronation in the late fourteenth century. Most significant in these respects was the reign of Richard II (1377–99). Crowned when aged 11, his spiritual aspirations for monarchy are reflected in contemporary painting (fig. 6) and were memorably recreated in the poetry of Shakespeare's history play:

> Not all the water in the rough rude sea
> Can wash the balm off from an anointed king;
> The breath of worldly men cannot depose
> The deputy elected by the Lord.
>
> *Richard II*, Act 3, Scene 2

By the fifteenth century the court was drawing up its own form of documentation for the procedure at coronations concerned primarily with recording the rights and duties of those holding the high offices of state or serving in the royal household. Its emphasis on ceremonial is in keeping with the importance attached to chivalry during the fifteenth century.

There was also, on occasions, a need to revise the liturgy and this task was usually undertaken by the Archbishop of Canterbury. Careful preparations in this respect were made for the coronation of Queen Anne (1714) by Archbishop Thomas Tenison and also by Archbishop Cosmo Lang for King George VI's coronation in 1937. Lang had preached at the coronation of King George V (1911), and now solemnly read his way through the relevant historical literature. He was deeply conscious of the sensitivities following the abdication

crisis of 1936 and accordingly he prepared both King George VI and Queen Elizabeth, as well as the nation, carefully for their coronation.

Some coronations were recorded in elaborately printed illustrated accounts. Of these, *The History of the Coronation of the Most High, Most Mighty, and Most Excellent Monarch James II ... on 23 April ... 1685* by Francis Sandford (1687) is illustrated with numerous engravings (fig. 7). *Ceremonial of the Coronation of His Most Sacred Majesty King George the Fourth* by John Whittaker (1823), later re-issued in a more manageable popular edition by Sir George Nayler (1837; fig. 8), is a deluxe publication, printed in gold, of which only six copies were issued. George IV's coronation in 1821 had been a lavish spectacle that cost £238,238 as compared with his father's in 1761 (£70,000), William IV's in 1831 (£42,298) or Queen Victoria's in 1838 (£69,421).

The costs of any coronation relate not just to the religious service itself but also to the events surrounding the ceremony. One of these was the Vigil Procession that was part of the spiritual preparation for the monarch before coronation day. The first recorded instance of the Vigil Procession, which went from the Tower of London to Westminster on the eve of the coronation, was in the reign of Richard II. That of Edward VI (r.1547–53) was particularly important since it followed Henry VIII's establishment of the Church of England (fig. 9), whilst that of Charles II was a statement of restored royal power viewed with some excitement by Pepys and Evelyn. The Vigil Procession

Fig. 7 'A Perspective of Westminster Abbey from the High-Altar to the West End shewing the Manner of His Majestie's Crowning', from Francis Sandford's *The History of the Coronation of the Most High, Most Mighty, and Most Excellent Monarch James II ... on 23 April ... 1685*, published in London by Thomas Newcomb, 1687
Etching, 38 × 50.5 cm (15 × 19¾")
Royal Collection (RCIN 1046687)

Sandford provides a highly detailed and richly illustrated description of the coronation of James II. The King was crowned with his Queen Consort, Mary of Modena, whom he had married in 1673: she is seen on the left in this print.

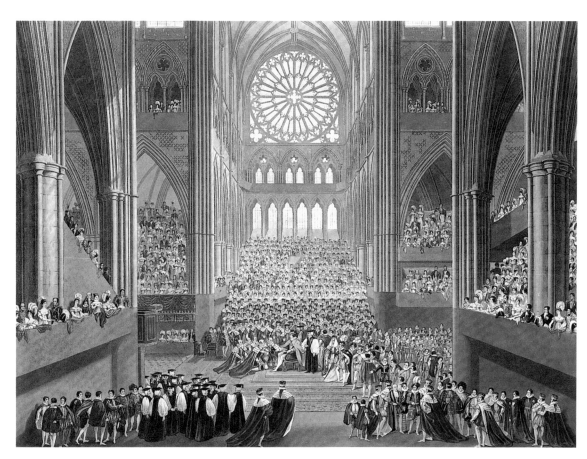

Fig. 8 'The Ceremony of the Homage', plate 39 from Sir George Nayler's *The Coronation of His Most Sacred Majesty King George the Fourth*, published in London by Henry George Bohn, 1837
Aquatint, 42.3 × 57.2 cm (16⅝ × 22½")
Royal Collection (RCIN 1051582)

The images in this book are an invaluable source for the spectacular scenes associated with George IV's coronation both in Westminster Abbey and at the banquet afterwards in Westminster Hall.

Fig. 9 James Basire (1730–1802), after Samuel
Hieronymus Grimm (1733–94)
*The Procession of King Edward VI From the Tower of London to
Westminster, Febr. XIX, MDXLVII, Previous to his Coronation,* 1788
Engraving for the Society of Antiquaries, 75.4 × 152.2 cm
(29$^{11}$/$_{16}$ × 59$^{15}$/$_{16}$″)
Royal Collection (RCIN 751246)

Edward VI was aged nine at his coronation. The Vigil
Procession was punctuated by pageants, speeches and
music, but otherwise was fairly restrained. The print
is based on a sixteenth-century mural formerly in the
Dining Parlour at Cowdray House in Sussex. The
subjects of the four other murals in the room were
scenes from Henry VIII's war against the French during
the 1540s. The murals were all destroyed by fire in the
eighteenth century.

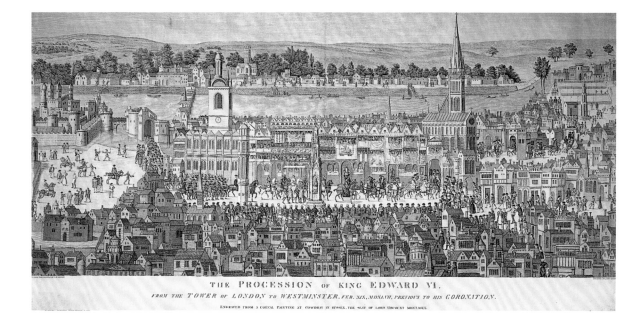

THE PROCESSION of KING EDWARD VI.
FROM THE TOWER TO LONDON TO WESTMINSTER, FEB. XIX, MDXLVII, PREVIOUS TO HIS CORONATION.
ENGRAVED FROM A COEVAL PAINTING AT COWDRAY IN SUSSEX, THE SEAT OF LORD VISCOUNT MONTAGUE.

in its most elaborate form did not continue after the
seventeenth century and the personal preparation by
the sovereign for the coronation became less demon-
strative and more private, with St James's Palace
and later Buckingham Palace as the focus. Since the
seventeenth century formal processions to the Abbey
have started first at Westminster Hall (until 1821) and
subsequently at Buckingham Palace.

A second event that continued for longer and was
certainly expensive to organise was the coronation
banquet in Westminster Hall. This assumed the form
of public dining and was observed by numerous
spectators. The climax was the appearance of the King's
Champion, who entered the Hall on horseback and
challenged anyone present to contest the sovereign's
right to rule. This role was traditionally taken by the
Dymoke family, who performed the office until the
coronation banquet of George IV, after which the tradition ceased. The painter Benjamin Robert Haydon

(1786–1846) witnessed this particular coronation banquet,
noting that it 'combined all the gorgeous splendour
of ancient chivalry with intense heroic interest of
modern times' and that the King 'looked like some
gorgeous bird of the East' (fig. 10).

Given their relative infrequency and the inherent
complications posed by the scale and length of the
proceedings, coronations were understandably accident-
prone. Mistakes were made, misunderstandings
occurred, and mishaps multiplied – mostly as a result
of the failure to record tradition or the lack of rehearsal.
From the modern period alone, George I's coronation
(1714) gave rise to a great deal of pushing and shoving
with important people breaking rank. The King's
Hanoverian origins meant that there were language
difficulties, so that the service had to be conducted in
dog Latin and French. Owing to a lack of rehearsals the
music was a disaster at the coronation of George II (1727).
The poet Thomas Gray (1716–71) witnessed the scene in

Fig. 10  George Jones (1786–1869)
*The Banquet at the Coronation of George IV, 19 July 1821*, 1821
Oil on canvas, 109.2 × 89.8 cm (43 × 35⅜″)
Royal Collection (RCIN 404463)

George IV is seated, robed and crowned, under a canopy on the royal platform at the far end of Westminster Hall. He raises his cup in acknowledgement of the King's Champion who is seen on horseback in full armour in the foreground, escorted by the Deputy Earl Marshal (Lord Howard of Effingham) and the Lord High Constable (the Duke of Wellington), both on horseback. The body of the Hall and the galleries above are filled with spectators.

Westminster Hall at George III's coronation (1761) and recorded mismanagement and near chaos both at the start, as the processions formed up before entering the Abbey, and afterwards at the banquet. In fact, it was not unusual for the coronation banquet to end in serious looting and pillaging in Westminster Hall by guests and spectators alike. Mrs Arbuthnot, the friend of the Duke of Wellington, objected to George IV ogling his mistress Lady Conyngham during the ceremony, which took place on a hot July day in 1821, and Lady Cowper reflected that the sovereign looked 'more like the Victim than the Hero of the Fête'. He used no less than nineteen pocket handkerchiefs to wipe the perspiration from his face during the enthroning alone as a result of the heat and his heavy garments (fig. 11). After the expense of George IV's coronation William IV's economies allowed for only a 'half-Crownation' (1831) with no processions and no banquet. At Queen Victoria's coronation (1838) there was a great deal of uncertainty about procedures, particularly amongst the clergy, culminating in the Archbishop of Canterbury forcing the sovereign's ring onto the wrong finger of the Queen's hand. Removing the ring afterwards in iced water proved painful. At the start of King Edward VII's coronation in 1902 the traditional anthem 'I was glad when they said unto me, We will go into the House of the Lord' (Psalm 122), in a new setting by Sir Hubert Parry, had to be sung twice because the signal that the King had arrived was given too early.

Some of these mishaps were interpreted in symbolic terms. A precious stone is said to have fallen from George III's crown while he moved around the Abbey and this was thought to have foretold the loss of the American colonies twenty-one years later. Thus, in such ways the numinous was tempered by reality. The omens, however, for the Coronation of Queen Elizabeth II were good. At the age of eleven The Queen had observed King George VI's coronation (12 May 1937) with a keen eye:

Then came Papa [King George VI] looking very beautiful in a crimson robe and the Cap of State.

Then the service began.

I thought it all <u>very</u>, <u>very</u> wonderful and I expect the Abbey did too. The arches and beams at the top were covered with a sort of haze of wonder as Papa was crowned, at least I thought so.

When Mummy [Queen Elizabeth] was crowned and all the peeresses put on their coronets it looked wonderful to see arms and coronets hovering in the air and then the arms disappear as if by magic. Also the music was lovely and the band, the orchestra and the new organ all played beautifully.

What struck me as being rather odd was that Grannie [Queen Mary] did not remember much of her own Coronation. I should have thought that it would have stayed in her mind for ever.

At the end the service got rather boring as it

Fig. 11 'The King In His Royal Robes wearing
a Cap of Estate', plate 34 from Sir George Nayler's
*The Coronation of His Most Sacred Majesty King George
the Fourth*, published in London by Henry George
Bohn, 1837
Aquatint, 42.3 × 57.5 cm (16⅝ × 22⅝")
Royal Collection (RCIN 1051582)

The costumes for the coronation of George IV were
based on Elizabethan and Jacobean styles, deliberately
evoking comparison with past history. Many of the
participants, including George IV, found the heat of
July to be overwhelming.

was all prayers. Grannie and I were looking to
see how many more pages to the end, and we
turned one more and then I pointed to the word
at the bottom of the page and it said 'Finis'. We
both smiled at each other and turned back to the
service.

After Papa had passed we were all shivering
because there was a most awful draught coming
from somewhere, so we were glad to get out
of the box. Then we went down the aisle, first a
gentleman I did not know, then Margaret and
myself and then Grannie. When we got back
to our dressing-room we had some sandwiches,
stuffed rolls, orangeade and lemonade.

*"Good! An excuse to dress up."*

# Coronation Day:
# Tuesday 2 June 1953

THE BREAKING DAWN did not augur well, as though the weather was conspiring against the occasion. Cecil Beaton (1904–80), who was due to take the official photographs in Buckingham Palace after the Coronation, rose very early like everyone else participating in the day's principal activities. He wrote in his diary, 'An angry wind blew the branches of the cherry tree in the next door garden, and despite the heavy sheets of rain people were already going off cheerfully and hurriedly to take their places in the crowd.' The unseasonable cold had not deterred vast crowds from sleeping out overnight in order to gain vantage points – an exercise that reminded many of the celebration of peace in 1945 after the Second World War (fig. 12). The Coronation of 1953 led to an invasion of the capital beginning on 23 May. People coming to see the decorations caused such traffic congestion that a ban had to be placed on private vehicles entering an area of a 3 kilometre (2 mile) radius from Westminster.

All those who experienced the early morning wait on the day refer to the air of mounting excitement both in the streets of London and in Westminster Abbey itself, where the doors closed to guests as early as 6.30 am. There then ensued a long wait of four hours or so during which those outside and in fortified themselves with coffee, sandwiches and sweets. From his position in the south transept Sir Henry Channon found that 'The long wait was enthralling as every few minutes a procession of distinguished guests, relations, minor royalties entered and were escorted to their seats … Dignitaries and ecclesiastics flittered about; peeresses got restive and retired to the Ladies' Room in red groups.' Those in the streets looked eagerly and expectantly for signs of the processions. The rain and the wind continued intermittently throughout the day, but would in the end only be regarded as incidental in the course of such dramatic events (fig. 13).

There was a great deal of waiting for participants and spectators alike while the dramatis personae forgathered. Each of the processions was carefully co-ordinated in order to facilitate seating or the taking up of positions in the Abbey (fig. 14). For example, the Lord Mayor's procession left the Mansion House at 7.55 am and the Speaker's procession from the House of Commons, which had to cover the shortest distance, followed much later at 9.30 am. Nothing was going to be allowed to disturb the careful planning that had been set in train in April 1952 under the direction of the Earl Marshal, an hereditary position held by the Dukes of Norfolk. Other key parties to the planning were the Lord Chamberlain's Office of the Royal Household, the Ministry of Works, and the Dean and Chapter of Westminster Abbey. Between them these different authorities had a whole range of responsibilities extending from the decorations and stands (fig. 15) along the processional routes and the strict protocol of the ceremonial to the entertainment of foreign visitors and the safety of the crowds. But it was the split-second timing that was crucial. Minor members of the

Fig. 12 *I am in The Mall — and they're all awake.*
From the *Daily Mail*, 2 June 1953, p.1

Crowds slept out overnight in damp
weather in order to reserve positions
for viewing the processions on
Coronation Day.

Fig. 13 *A Scurry of Peers*
From the *News Chronicle*, Coronation
Number, 3 June 1953, p.10

A group of peers photographed leaving
Westminster Abbey are caught in a
sudden squall. The weather singularly
failed to rise to the occasion and the sun
hardly shone at all on Coronation Day,
but the conditions did not dampen
people's spirits. *The Times* trumpeted on
the following day 'Processional Glory
Undimmed by Rain'.

# CORONATION PROCESSION
# OF HER MAJESTY QUEEN ELIZABETH II

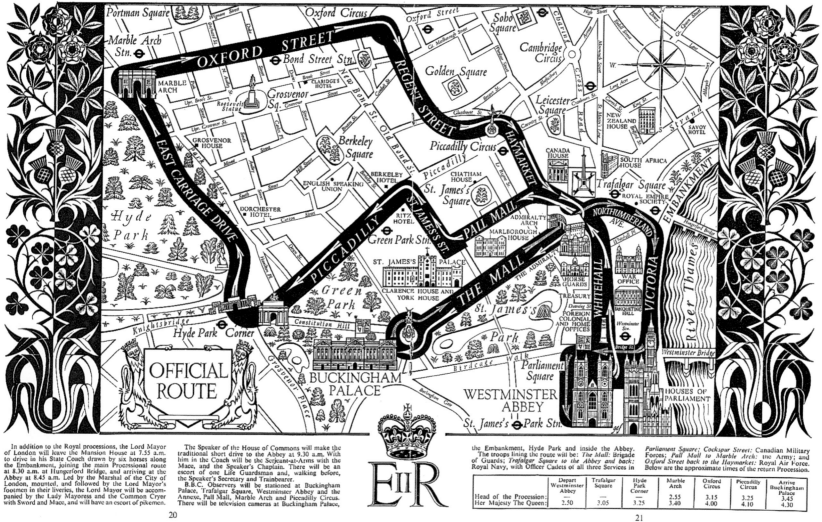

**OFFICIAL ROUTE**

In addition to the Royal processions, the Lord Mayor of London will leave the Mansion House at 7.55 a.m. to drive in his State Coach drawn by six horses along the Embankment, joining the main Processional route at 8.30 a.m. at Hungerford Bridge, and arriving at the Abbey at 8.45 a.m. Led by the Marshal of the City of London, mounted, and followed by the Lord Mayor's footmen in their liveries, the Lord Mayor will be accompanied by the Lady Mayoress and the Common Cryer with Sword and Mace, and will have an escort of pikemen.

The Speaker of the House of Commons will make the traditional short drive to the Abbey at 9.30 a.m. With him in the Coach will be the Serjeant-at-Arms with the Mace, and the Speaker's Chaplain. There will be an escort of one Life Guardsman and, walking before, the Speaker's Secretary and Trainbearer.

B.B.C. Observers will be stationed at Buckingham Palace, Trafalgar Square, Westminster Abbey and the Annexe, Pall Mall, Marble Arch and Piccadilly Circus. There will be television cameras at Buckingham Palace,

the Embankment, Hyde Park and inside the Abbey.

The troops lining the route will be: *The Mall:* Brigade of Guards; *Trafalgar Square to the Abbey and back:* Royal Navy, with Officer Cadets of all three Services in

*Parliament Square; Cockspur Street:* Canadian Military Forces; *Pall Mall to Marble Arch:* the Army; and *Oxford Street back to the Haymarket:* Royal Air Force. Below are the approximate times of the return Procession.

| | Depart Westminster Abbey | Trafalgar Square | Hyde Park Corner | Marble Arch | Oxford Circus | Piccadilly Circus | Arrive Buckingham Palace |
|---|---|---|---|---|---|---|---|
| Head of the Procession: | — | 3.05 | — | 2.55 | 3.15 | 3.25 | 3.45 |
| Her Majesty The Queen: | 2.50 | | 3.25 | 3.40 | 4.00 | 4.10 | 4.30 |

20

21

Fig. 14  *Coronation Procession of Her Majesty Queen Elizabeth II*
Printed map, 22.7 × 33.7 cm (8¹⁵⁄₁₆ × 13¼")
*From The Coronation of Her Majesty Queen Elizabeth II,*
approved souvenir programme, pp.20—21

The two main processional routes on Coronation Day differed in length. The shorter one before the service was from Buckingham Palace to Westminster Abbey. After the service the route for the return to the Palace was more elaborate. The 7.2 km (4½ miles) took the 16,000 participants two hours to complete. The column of some 10,000 troops, accompanied by 27 bands, stretched for 3 km: those on foot marched 10 abreast whilst those on horseback rode 6 abreast. The purpose of the extended route was so that The Queen and the processions could be seen by as many people as possible.

Stands were built at key points on the processional routes which were lined by nearly 6,000 troops together with police, as well as being decorated with 77,000 plants.

The principal decorations for the processional route were in The Mall where there were four twin-spanned arches of tubular steel with gilt latticed fan-shaped designs that were illuminated at night. The arches, designed by Eric Bedford, Chief Architect to the Ministry of Works, were 19 metres (65 feet) high and each was surmounted by two gold lions and two white unicorns 6 metres (20 feet) high, designed by James Woodford. Suspended from the centre of each of the arches on gilded wires was a 'Princess's coronet' intended to create a fairy-tale effect. The arches were linked by a series of flagpoles surmounted by crowns and each hung with four banners in red decorated with royal monograms.

Royal Family left Buckingham Palace at 8.40 am and members or representatives of foreign royalty departed from St James's Palace at 8.50 am. Colonial rulers rode out from Buckingham Palace at 9.15 am and the prime ministers of the United Kingdom and the Commonwealth at 9.20 am. Senior members of the Royal Family started to leave Buckingham Palace at 9.40 am and Queen Elizabeth The Queen Mother, accompanied by Princess Margaret, set out from Clarence House at 10.00 am. The climax of these processions was The Queen's, which passed through the gates of Buckingham Palace at 10.26 am and arrived at Westminster Abbey at 11 am, having progressed along The Mall and under Admiralty Arch before going across the south side of Trafalgar Square, and then along Northumberland Avenue, Victoria Embankment and Bridge Street before entering Parliament Square (fig.16). The Coronation service began at 11.15 am and lasted almost three hours, concluding at 2.00 pm.

The service started with the sovereign's procession from the specially built annexe at the west door of Westminster Abbey. This was long, numbering some 250 people representing crown, church and state. The regalia and the ecclesiastical vessels to be used in the

Fig. 17 *Six Stages of the Coronation*
From *Country Life Picture Book of the Coronation*,
Nos 26, 28, 29, 36, 38, 41.

service were each carried by a representative tradi-tionally designated for the task — St Edward's Crown by the Viscount Cunningham of Hyndhope, Lord High Steward; the Sword of State by the Marquess of Salisbury; and the Orb by the Earl Alexander of Tunis. The Queen wore the Diamond Diadem made for George IV, Queen Victoria's collet necklace and drop diamond earrings, together with the collar and badge of the Order of the Garter. Over the Coronation Dress she wore the crimson Robe of Parliament borne by the Maids of Honour. The procession made its way up the nave to the 'theatre'. This was sparsely furnished with St Edward's Chair and a throne on a gold carpet. The procession arrived at the 'theatre' to the sound of Parry's setting of Psalm 122 ('I was Glad') and to shouts of 'Vivat Regina Elizabetha', a full-throated sound led by the King's Scholars of Westminster School that recalled the primitive elements that still attach themselves to the occasion. The 'theatre' is aptly named and Cecil Beaton for one recognised its potential:

> The colours red, gold and smoke-blue always be-guiled one's eye by the unexpected. The brilliant gold carpet was the perfect floor-covering for the slippered feet of the pages, the train-bearers, and the scarlet, blue and gold-clad heralds, for the bishops and clergy in white and gold. Black Rod made way for a messenger; a mote of light caught a gold sequin fallen on the carpet, or a jewel in a bishop's ring; the sun came out and lit up a posse of scarlet uniformed Goldsticks. It was all living and new: it was history, but of today and of the future. It was something that is pulsating and vital to us, and an essential part of the life we believe in.

The Coronation service fell into six main parts (fig. 17) and was conducted by the Archbishop of Canterbury (Dr Geoffrey Fisher), supported by the Bishop of Durham (Dr A. M. Ramsay) and the Bishop of Bath and Wells (Dr H. W. Bradfield). First, the Recognition was repeated four times with The Queen facing north, south, west and east. The Archbishop said, 'Sirs, I here present unto you Queen Elizabeth, your undoubted Queen: Wherefore all you who are come this day to do your homage and service, Are you willing to do the same?' The congregation responded with the accla-mation 'God Save Queen Elizabeth.' Second, was the taking and signing of the Oath whereby the sovereign agrees to stay within the law, to maintain the Church of England, and to exercise justice and mercy. This was followed by the Presentation of the Bible, an act which allowed for the participation of the Moderator of the General Assembly of the Church of Scotland (Dr J. Pitt Watson) in the service for the first time.

The third and central act was the Anointing of the sovereign, which was preceded by communion. The Anointing took place under a canopy of cloth-of-gold held by four Knights of the Order of the Garter. For this The Queen was seated on St Edward's Chair and divested of all the symbols of wealth and power, putting on a plain white muslin dress as a symbolic act, while the choir sang G. F. Handel's anthem *Zadok the Priest*, originally composed for George II's coronation. The combination of the act of Anointing with this par-ticular music was one of the most affecting parts of the service.

The Crowning — the fourth part — was the climax to a series of acts investing the sovereign with the royal regalia. Robed in a white sleeveless garment (the *colobium sindonis*) under another garment of gold (the *supertunica*), The Queen, still seated in St Edward's Chair, was presented with the golden spurs signifying chivalry and the jewelled sword symbolising justice. The newly made armills (bracelets), representing sincerity and wisdom, were then clasped around her wrists. For the Crowning she put on the stole and the cloth-of-gold robe known as the Imperial Mantle (*pallium regale*), and received the symbols of royal authority. The first of these was the orb, symbolising independent sovereignty under the Cross. Next came the coronation ring (known as the 'wedding ring of England'), symbolising faith, and the glove worn on the right hand, symbolising good governance. There followed the two rods — in the right hand the sceptre with the Cross signifying power and justice, and in the left the rod with the dove representing equity and mercy. The congregation now stood for the Crowning itself. St Edward's Crown, which had been previously

placed on the high altar, was held aloft by the Archbishop of Canterbury before being lowered onto The Queen's head, at which point there was a further acclamation of 'God Save The Queen' accompanied by a trumpet fanfare and the sounding of guns at the Tower of London. At the same time in the Abbey the congregation surrounding the 'theatre' put on their coronets and caps of state in a flurry of movement – 'the peeresses, with long, gloved arms looking like wishbones', according to Beaton. The Crowning was followed by the Benediction, the words of which referred not to the Empire, as in 1937, but to the Commonwealth. Moving from St Edward's Chair to the throne The Queen was formally enthroned, so that in the sixth part of the ceremony homage could be paid by the Archbishop of Canterbury representing the Lords Spiritual, then by The Duke of Edinburgh as the sovereign's consort, and finally by the royal princes and members of the peerage, the Lords Temporal. The service ended with the completion of communion culminating in the singing of the Te Deum. At this point The Queen retired to St Edward's Chapel for a recess before the final procession from the Abbey. St Edward's Crown was now exchanged for the Imperial State Crown, and carrying both the orb and the sceptre, The Queen processed out of the Abbey wearing the embroidered purple velvet Robe of Estate over the Coronation Dress while the congregation sang the National Anthem. The procession mirrored in reverse that which had occurred on arrival in the Abbey three hours earlier. On both occasions The Queen's measured tread was distinctive and Beaton described it: 'As she walks she allows her heavy skirts to swing backwards and forwards in a beautiful rhythmic effect. This girlish figure has enormous dignity; she belongs in this scene of almost Byzantine magnificence.' Channon, no doubt like many others, commented, 'I could have watched for ever. The red, the gold, the sparkle, the solemnity…'

There was more waiting at the end of the ceremony. Only after the return procession had been formed up could those in the Abbey, who had been in their seats since early morning, be released. Even so, this had to be done in an orderly way. Channon records that 'People were let out in batches, and as our numbers were called out by a loud speaker, there was some indignation amongst MPs at the delay.' Others were more philosophical – 'What had been an honour to endure for The Queen had become only an imposition now that it was done at the behest of some unknown official,' wrote Brigadier Stanley Clark. The return procession, which set out at 2.30 pm, incorporated all the elements that had arrived separately at the Abbey before the service but these were augmented by additional troops and bands. The route, too, was longer, leading up Whitehall, across the south side of Trafalgar Square, along Pall Mall and up St James's Street into Piccadilly, towards Hyde Park Corner and then along the East Carriage Drive on the edge of Hyde Park (see fig. 14). After passing under Marble Arch the procession turned into Oxford Street, following it down into Regent Street and Haymarket, recrossing Trafalgar Square for the third and last time before passing under Admiralty Arch and returning along The Mall to Buckingham Palace, where The Queen arrived at 4.30 pm. It was at this stage that Cecil Beaton (fig. 18) and other official photographers took their formal photographs in the Green Drawing Room and the Throne Room respectively. The Queen, Beaton noticed, 'looked extremely minute under her robes and Crown, her nose and hands chilled and her eyes tired'.

The crowds gathered around the Victoria Memorial for the appearances by the Royal Family on the balcony of the palace and a flypast by the Royal Air Force. There were five appearances in all, the last in evening dress. During the course of the evening The Queen broadcast to the nation, introduced by the Prime Minister, Sir Winston Churchill:

The ceremonies you have seen today are ancient, and some of their origins are veiled in the mists of the past. But their spirit and their meaning shine through the ages – never, perhaps, more brightly than now. I have in sincerity pledged myself to your service, as so many of you are pledged to mine …

… I have behind me not only the splendid traditions and the annals of more than a thousand years but the living strength and majesty of the Commonwealth and Empire: of societies old

Fig. 18 Cecil Beaton (1904–80)
*Queen Elizabeth II after the Coronation,*
*2 June 1953*

Numerous official photographs were
taken in Buckingham Palace after the
Coronation, but the most memorable are
those by Cecil Beaton. For his defining
image he posed The Queen in front of a
backdrop depicting Henry VII's Chapel in
Westminster Abbey. Beaton wrote a vivid
account of this historic photographic
session in his published *Diary* (1979).

and new, of lands and races different in history and origins, but all, by God's will, united in spirit and in aim.

Therefore I am sure that this, my Coronation, is not the symbol of a power and a splendour that are gone but a declaration of our hopes for the future, and for the years I may, by God's grace and mercy, be given to reign and serve you as your Queen.

The palace was floodlit from 9.45 pm until 11.30 pm and the celebrations culminated in a firework display on the River Thames opposite the Royal Festival Hall beginning at 10.30 pm. That concluded Coronation Day, but The Queen then undertook further engagements in London, Scotland and Northern Ireland, as well as an extensive tour of the Commonwealth lasting for six months, from 23 November 1953 to 15 May 1954. Meanwhile, the furnishings in the Abbey specially made for the Coronation were sold, following established practice.

The Coronation impressed itself upon the historical consciousness of the nation through a range of diverse associations. The first ascent of Everest – the highest peak in the world – was made by a Common-wealth expedition on 29 May 1953 and this success was announced four days later on the morning of the Coronation (fig. 19). The conquest of Everest was regarded as a good omen for the new reign. This

mood of optimism was underscored by the accession of a young radiant queen aged 27 (in 1838 Queen Victoria had been 19) who was seen as a symbol of hope and regeneration after the Second World War.

A feeling of national resurgence had already been set in train by the Festival of Britain held in 1951, but this was not – and could not be – a reaffirmation of the British Empire, just as it was too early for the country to commit itself to any new international alliance. To a certain extent for the British, the combination of a post-war vacuum of power in Europe and the decline of imperial greatness led to a re-assessment of the Commonwealth. As the political historian Ben Pimlott has expressed it, 'The Coronation provided an opportunity to display a new kind of imperial greatness, by reaffirming the Monarchy as a cord tying together the Empire and Commonwealth into a group of diplomatically, economically and even militarily associated nations.' The processions at the Coronation of 1953 reflected the changing status of Britain in the world order. It may have been in Pimlott's words 'the last great imperial display, a magnificent funeral tribute to a world order that was ending', but it also contained within it the possibilities for future development.

If The Queen was the symbol of change, Sir Winston Churchill was its spokesman (fig. 20). Returned to power in 1951 for a second term as Prime Minister at the age of 77, he immediately recognised the implications of a young sovereign at this juncture in the country's

Fig. 19 *On the Summit. Tensing, photographed by his companion Hillary, at 11.30 a.m. on Friday, May 29, 1953* From *The Times*, First Ascent of Mount Everest Supplement, July 1953, cover

The summit of Mount Everest, 8,850 metres (29,030 feet) high, was reached by Edmund Hillary, a New Zealander, and Sherpa Tensing Bhutia on 29 May and was reported in *The Times* on the morning of the Coronation. The ascent had been undertaken by a British team of climbers sponsored by the Royal Geographical Society with the Alpine Club. Hillary and Tensing spent fifteen minutes on the summit planting a string of flags and taking photographs. The conquest of Everest after numerous attempts by earlier expeditions was described as 'a victory for the human spirit'.

history. In a speech at a dinner in Westminster Hall six days before the Coronation in the presence of The Queen, Churchill emphasised the role that monarchy played in providing 'the central link in all our modern changing life ... the one which above all others claims our allegiance to death'. Churchill had been an inspirational figure for the British people during the Second World War and his own career extended as far back as the reign of Queen Victoria. The admiration felt by him personally for The Queen ('the young, gleaming champion') was undoubtedly reciprocated, and Churchill had been invested with the Order of the Garter in April 1953.

The sense of regeneration and the dawn of a new Elizabethan age was underlined by a special production at the Old Vic of Shakespeare's late history play (c.1613) *Henry VIII*. This had also been revived at the time of the coronation of George II (1727) and was popular on state occasions because of its use of ceremonial in the plot. Act 4, Scene 1 incorporates a procession following the coronation of Anne Boleyn and the closing scene of the play (Act 5, Scene 4) is the christening of the future Elizabeth I – a moment of particular significance therefore in 1953. The Queen and Prince Philip attended a gala performance at the Old Vic on the evening of 6 May, and met the cast afterwards (fig. 21) – Paul Rogers (Henry VIII), Gwen Ffrangcon-Davies (Catherine of Aragon) and Alexander Knox (Wolsey).

The same spirit of optimism was given musical expression by Benjamin Britten's three-act opera

Fig. 20 *Sir Winston Churchill ... leaves 10 Downing Street for the Abbey* From *Country Life Picture Book of the Coronation*, No.5

As Conservative Prime Minister Sir Winston Churchill (1874–1965) played a pivotal role in preparing the country for the Coronation in the aftermath of the Second World War. He repeatedly reinforced the significance of monarchy and its position at the apex of the social hierarchy. For the ceremony he wore the uniform of the Warden of the Cinque Ports with the robes of the Order of the Garter, the star of which had belonged to the former Foreign Secretary Viscount Castlereagh (1769–1822), and had subsequently passed into Churchill family ownership.

Fig. 21 *Her Majesty meets a famous predecessor. At a gala performance of* King Henry VIII *she is shown chatting to Paul Rogers, who took the name part in the play.* From *The Queen Elizabeth Coronation Souvenir*, 1953

The most important roles in *Henry VIII* were those of Cardinal Wolsey and Catherine of Aragon, although the part of the King was also strongly cast. The play was frequently performed during earlier centuries, often in lavish productions, but it did not have such an appeal for modern audiences. The production in 1953 was directed by Sir Tyrone Guthrie who had directed the play on two previous occasions. The Royal Shakespeare Company revived the play again in 1969/70 and 1983. The production specially staged in Coronation year allowed for such photo-opportunities as the real Queen Elizabeth II face-to-face with a costumed Henry VIII.

Photograph © Roger Wood

Fig. 22 *Gloriana* at Covent Garden

Of the operas composed by Benjamin Britten for the stage *Gloriana* is perhaps the least well-known. In the sequence of his operatic compositions it follows *Peter Grimes* (1945), *The Rape of Lucretia* (1946), *Albert Herring* (1947) and *Billy Budd* (1951). It preceded *The Turn of the Screw* (1954), written for La Fenice, Venice, work on which had to be postponed because of *Gloriana*. The opera was composed very fast, in six months, and extracts were played to The Queen privately on 18 May at the London home of Lord and Lady Harewood. The principal parts were taken by Joan Cross as Elizabeth I and Peter Pears as the Earl of Essex. The dances in the opera were specially choreographed by John Cranko; the sets were by John Piper and the premiere was conducted by John Pritchard.

*Gloriana*, specially commissioned by the Royal Opera House where The Queen's cousin the 7th Earl of Harewood was a Director (fig. 22). The premiere at Covent Garden was on 8 June, but it was not an outstanding success. Britten (1913–76), together with his librettist, William Plomer (1903–73), wrote the opera around the story of Elizabeth I and the Earl of Essex, using Lytton Strachey's book of 1928 as their point of departure. For most of the audience the opera was too introspective in its examination of the interplay between the public and private responsibilities of the protagonists. Opinions also varied about the music. Some thought it was a pastiche and others found it too subtle or not suitably rousing for such a prestigious

occasion. Words such as 'Boriana' or 'Yawniana' were bandied about, although not all the critics were dismissive. Part of the problem at the opening gala performance was people's expectations. The critic Philip Hope-Wallace wrote, 'As the audience turned towards the royal box and the National Anthem crashed out from the orchestra, it seemed as if one of those legendary nights of the Edwardian golden age of opera had come again. But in those days a royal gala would have meant titbits from *Aida* or *Bohème*. Tonight we were to see and hear a completely new opera.' In a letter to *The Times* (18 June 1955), the composer Ralph Vaughan Williams (1872–1958) asserted that this was 'the first time in history' that a British sovereign had commissioned an opera by a British composer. Britten was made a Companion of Honour in the Coronation Honours List and *Gloriana* itself has since won more considered plaudits. As Andrew Porter perceptively wrote at the time, *Gloriana* is 'a work of great imagination and power ... an opera remarkable for its truth to history, for its effect in the theatre and for the unfailing interest of its music'.

Sir William Walton (1902–83) wrote music that was more generally acceptable to the wider public. Walton had already composed *Crown Imperial* for the coronation of King George VI in 1937 and he contributed a similar piece, *Sceptre and Orb*, for the ceremony in 1953 – both titles taken from one of the King's soliloquies before the Battle of Agincourt in Shakespeare's *Henry V* (Act 4, Scene 1). Walton was also commissioned to compose a new setting for the Te Deum that was sung after the communion in the Coronation service. Traditionally, the Te Deum, like several of the other pieces of music that had over the centuries come to be associated with the service, was always sung to a new setting written specially for each coronation. In addition to Walton, Arnold Bax, George Dyson, Sir William Harris, Herbert Howells, Healey Willan and Vaughan Williams were invited to contribute or make new arrangements for the service. Otherwise, much of the music by Handel, Samuel Wesley and Sir Charles Stanford was retained from previous coronations. The combined choirs numbered 400 voices supplemented by 60 orchestral players.

Quite apart from individual contributions, the Coronation of 1953 was memorable for one major technological advance – the use of television. Whilst the coronation of King George V in 1911 had been photographed and extensively reported in the press and that in 1937 of King George VI had been broadcast on radio with restricted filming in the Abbey, the Coronation of 1953 was the first to be televised. This turned it into an event of universal appeal and the live transmission of such an important ceremony amounted to a revolution in the use of modern media. A television link-up with countries in Europe – France, West Germany, Holland – and the showing of a telerecording in America only a few hours after the event itself meant that the Coronation of Queen Elizabeth II was a widely witnessed event.

There were considerable social implications in this. For many the Coronation became a shared, all-inclusive experience. Owners of television sets were relatively few in number and people therefore hired sets for the occasion, so enabling them to invite friends into their homes specially to see the coverage. This added to the feeling of participation, kindling a community spirit, and through that an affirmation of national identity. An estimated 27 million people watched the Coronation live on television in Britain, or at least part of it, since the broadcast covering the whole day lasted for twelve hours. After a concerted campaign by the BBC, licence holders doubled from 1½ million to 3 million just before Coronation Day, and very many of those who hired sets retained them. For most people it was the first time that they had seen television, which from this moment became a dominant and influential force in everyday life. Ironically, The Queen was not at first keen to grant permission for the service to be televised, regarding the cameras as intrusive in their relentless gaze both from a distance and in potentially more intimate close-ups. There was also a fear that any mistakes or mishaps would be all too clearly apparent and recorded for posterity. In the end The Queen overcame her reservations, appreciating that there were considerable advantages in a televised broadcast. Agreement was reached with the BBC on matters of editorial policy and on the location of appropriate fixed camera positions (fig. 23). A list of procedures was duly drawn up and punctiliously

observed. The Anointing, for instance, was not to be filmed. The Coronation of 1953 was, in essence, the first television spectacular and the fact that it involved monarchy was not without significance for later developments. This first extended outside broadcast set high standards with a strong cast of commentators led by Richard Dimbleby (supported, amongst others, by Bernard Braden, Sylvia Peters and Brian Johnston) and it became a touchstone for future programmes (fig. 24). According to Pimlott, what this first television broadcast amounted to was 'a baptism for a new kind of mass participation in national events, which changed for ever the way in which royalty would be perceived'.

There were, in addition, many other lesser innovations on Coronation Day. No doubt the periscopes used by the crowds lining the route in order to see over the heads of those standing in front were an improvement on previous models. More famously, there was a culinary breakthrough. The foreign guests who were to be entertained in the Great Hall of Westminster School after the Coronation required feeding and for that purpose food had to be prepared in advance. Constance Spry (1886–1960), who was also responsible for some of the floral arrangements on the day, proposed a recipe of cold chicken in a curry cream sauce, with a well-seasoned dressed salad of rice, green peas and mixed herbs as a suitable collation. This idea was made possible by the development of modern refrigerators, which were almost as scarce as televisions. Once cooked the food could be safely stored

## You can follow it all on this Abbey plan

**Camera positions**

HENRY VII's CHAPEL

**11.25 A.M.**

NORTH TRANSEPT — THEATRE — SOUTH TRANSEPT

TRIFORIUM

ORGAN SCREEN

**11.15 A.M.**

NAVE

WEST DOOR

**11.0 A.M.**

THE ANNEXE

### THEATRE PLAN

ST EDWARD'S CHAPEL

HIGH ALTAR — CHAIR OF ESTATE

CORONATION CHAIR

ROYAL BOX

THE THRONE

Before the Queen's arrival at 11 a.m. the camera in the Abbey ANNEXE will record the arrival of the Royal Family, of the peers and Prime Ministers, and all others taking part in the Abbey procession. The camera over the great WEST DOOR will look down as the procession goes by. The camera over the ORGAN SCREEN will look towards the High Altar to pick out such moments as the Recognition, and that in the SOUTH TRANSEPT will show the peers in Homage. The camera in the TRIFORIUM above the High Altar will look down on the Coronation theatre where the Queen will be crowned. It is from this position that Richard Dimbleby will describe the service.

Fig. 23  *You can follow it all on this Abbey plan*
From *Coronation TV Express*, n.d., p.11

The televising of the Coronation by the BBC was a breakthrough in the history of outside broadcasting. Careful negotiations with Buckingham Palace resulted in an agreed list of procedures involving the placement of cameras, the framing of shots, and restrictions on the use of close-ups. This diagram shows the position of the cameras in Westminster Abbey.

## WATCH BY THE CLOCK

**ROBERT CANNELL** *gives you a camera's-eye timetable of the day's great moments.*

SYLVIA PETERS

MARY MALCOLM

**10.15 A.M.** Outside Buckingham Palace: a TV camera on the Palace roof gazes down on the crowded Mall. Another on the Victoria Memorial gives closer views.

**10.26 A.M.** The Queen drives forth with her husband, the Duke of Edinburgh, and the jingling, glittering Sovereign's Escort of cavalry. TV's cameras and microphones send out the first mighty roar of London's greeting.

**10.32 A.M.** Over to Westminster Abbey to see Queen Elizabeth the Queen Mother arrive.

**10.45 A.M.** Now the children of London welcome their Queen as she drives along the Embankment.

**11 A.M.** Back to the Abbey. High above the streets a TV camera catches the first glimpse of the procession swinging round Parliament-square. As the State Coach slows to halt by the Annexe, the picture changes to that from the camera stationed by the door.

The Queen steps down, her maids arrange her train, and then follow her into the Abbey.

Inside the Abbey still more cameras screen the slow, dignified procession up the great nave and into the central space where the Coronation Service begins.

Although more than half the congregation will now have to follow the Service by ear, we, the people, watch through the eyes of TV, ensconced in hidden cubicles.

**12.30 P.M.** Now the great moment — THE CROWNING, the tremendous moment when the Archbishop of Canterbury gently places the Crown on the Queen's head.

We see the flash and gleam of a thousand coronets being put on by the peers and peeresses. We see and hear the first acclaim by the representatives of the people, the Queen's Scholars of Westminster School, as they shout "Vivat Regina."

During the Service of Holy Communion the TV eye fixes on the altar. The commentators' voices are stilled. For this is the holy moment where none may intrude.

And so to the ending of the Abbey services at 1.50 p.m. and the procession of the new-crowned Queen down the nave to the Jerusalem Chamber.

BERKELEY SMITH
Outside the Palace.

MARY HILL
Outside the Abbey.

MAX ROBERTSON
Victoria Embankment

RICHARD DIMBLEBY
In the Abbey.

**2.20 P.M.** Outside the Abbey we see the marshalling of the giant array.

**2.50 P.M.** The march begins with thousands of Empire and Commonwealth troops, official representatives, and civilians escorting their Queen through her capital to her Palace.

**3.40 P.M.** The Queen passes cameras at Grosvenor Gate. And during this long march we see the entire parade twice—once from each side of the road.

**4.30 P.M.** The Queen returns to Buckingham Palace—and TV brings us close to the Royal Family, including Prince Charles and Princess Anne, as they make the traditional appearance on the balcony.

And for the first time Britain has a royal view of these wonderful scenes through the TV camera posted on the Palace roof, looking down on the throng.

**5 P.M.** TV makes ready for the great salute by the R.A.F.

**5.15 P.M.** Over London they come . . . thundering across the roof tops and swinging round in salute across St. James's and Green Parks.

BRIAN JOHNSTON
Grosvenor Gate.

**5.20 P.M.** The greatest TV programme of all signs off, and we return to Lime-grove, where children from all over Britain celebrate by staging a studio Tattoo, the first ever, with bands, marching, and gymnastic displays.

**8 P.M.** A telefilm of parts of the morning's Service in Westminster Abbey.

**8.55 P.M.** Sir Winston Churchill, the Prime Minister, introduces the Queen (sound only).

**9 P.M.** The Queen speaks to her peoples (sound only).

**9.10 P.M.** Outside Buckingham Palace we see the rejoicings and, possibly, another appearance by the Queen and Prince Philip on the balcony.

**9.20 P.M.** TV Newsreel, Coronation edition': the film cameras stationed along the route during the day tell the pavement story of the processions.

**10.20 P.M.** Coronation Night on the Thames: cameras join the crowds along the river at Westminster to watch the great fireworks display rounding off the day.

**11.30 P.M.** Weather forecast and news (sound only).

BERNARD BRADEN
Grosvenor Gate.

Fig. 24  *WATCH BY THE CLOCK*
From *Coronation TV Express*, n.d., p.11

The head of the BBC's outside broadcasting was S. J. de Lotbinière with Peter Dimmock as his assistant. All the commentators went on to become household names in their own right and Richard Dimbleby in particular built up a reputation for commentating on state occasions.

Fig. 25 *Queen Salote of Tonga*
From *Picture Post*, Special Coronation Souvenir Number,
Vol.59, No.11, 13 June 1953, p.59

Queen Salote of Tonga (1900–65) was universally admired
for remaining undaunted by the rain throughout the
long procession after the Coronation service and refusing
to raise the roof of her carriage. At 1.87 metres (6 ft 2 in)
tall and dressed in the robes of the Order of the British
Empire over her national costume, Queen Salote was
a formidable presence. She shared a carriage with the
Sultan of Kelanton who was accordingly very damp by
the end.

until needed. Constance Spry's recipe won the approval
of the Minister of Works, David Eccles, and has ever since
been known as Coronation Chicken (see page 94).

Not everything went perfectly on the day. The
weather was recalcitrant, although Queen Salote of
Tonga pleased the crowds by refusing to be daunted by
the rain and made choreographic use of her umbrella
(fig. 25). More dramatically, during the return procession Sir Winston Churchill's carriage was brought to

a halt by a traffic-jam and had to return to Downing
Street – but not before he had waved to The Queen
as she passed by in the Gold State Coach.

Sir Henry Channon reflected in his diary at the end
of the long day, 'What a day for England, and the traditional forces of the world. Shall we ever see the like
again? I have been present at two Coronations and now
shall never see another. Will my Paul [his son] be an old
man at that of King Charles III?'

# 'The artist as the eye of history':
# Feliks Topolski (1907–89)

THE LIFE OF FELIKS TOPOLSKI (fig. 26) spanned nearly the whole of the twentieth century. He witnessed and recorded most of its horrors, becoming thereby an unforgettable chronicler of his age, but at the same time he viewed his fellow human beings with compassion, understanding and humour. The vigour of his work signifies a sense of urgency and yet also a certain play-fulness. The insistency of his line similarly denotes a sense of purpose, just as his tireless eye and busy hand were in thrall to the ceaseless change that charac-terised one of the most dramatic centuries in history.

The energy of Topolski's style is indicative also of his restless spirit, expressed mainly in his frequent travels. Like Odysseus, he roamed the world and the visual records of his trips to India, Burma, China, Europe, the Middle East, North and South America, the Caribbean and Africa, amongst numerous other places, became one of the mainstays of his art. This fascination with the variety of life was matched by an uncanny ability to be in the right place at the right time, so that his work takes on an historical dimension as a form of sophisticated reportage. Again in this respect the vitality of the style mirrors the anxieties of the age.

Feliks Topolski was born in Poland in 1907. His father, Edward Topolski, was an actor and his mother was Stanislawa Drutowska, whose family came from the industrial city of Łódź. Both were political activists at a time of rising Polish nationalism. Topolski was trained as an artist at the Academy in Warsaw and quickly established a reputation for himself as a painter and illustrator with further interests in theatre and film. An early mural – a type of painting he returned to later in his life – was commissioned in 1934 by the Polish Institute for the Promotion of Modern Art (IPS) in Warsaw. Topolski's training as an artist was combined with a stint as a cadet in the Officers' School of Artillery Reserve where he relished the elaborate uniforms and parades on horseback.

These early experiences in Poland were clearly forma-tive for Topolski. As the art historian Bernard Denvir has expressed it, 'Growing up beneath the shadow of Warsaw's rococo architecture and revelling in the new-found nationalism of Marshal Pilsudski's Poland were both experiences which were to have a deep influence on his personality, endowing him with a taste for the rhetorical flourish, a liking for dash, a penchant for pageant and ceremonial.' These experiences were ex-tended in 1933 by travel in France and Italy, which the artist described as stepping 'out of Central Europe's sameness into uniqueness'. Two years later, Topolski was sent to Britain by a Polish journal to report on the Silver Jubilee of King George V and Queen Mary. He was entranced by what he saw and wrote in his idiosyncratic autobiography *Fourteen Letters* (1988):

The worldwide manhood's snobbery over 'Old England' paraphernalia made the visitor melt towards the sporty/tweedy/Burberry/Lock/Brigg realities. But there was more: their spindly posturings; their sartorial unerring subtleties – out of uniform and in (not excluding the field-cum-tropics uniforms, blend with safari eccentricities, flourishing in distant campaignings) – all perfectly in accord with their long-boned pear-shapes; with the land's greenness and Georgian bricks' blackness of London and the interwoven red.

Topolski duly settled in London and became a British citizen in 1947. Following his marriage firstly in 1944 to Marion Everall, by whom he had two children (Daniel and Teresa) and secondly in 1975 to Caryl Stanley, family life became an added element in his art.

Geography always played an important part in Topolski's work, but essentially it is human geography. He was an acute observer of national characteristics, but beneath the surface of his subjects he recognised a shared comedy of manners that became the focus of his attention. To a certain extent Topolski remained an exile, adopting the perspective of an outsider, and this sharpened his powers of observation. He retained the characteristics of a central European so that while his ebullient style can be equated with his mercurial temperament, the humour is often tinged with melancholy. Topolski, however, was not simply an observer and passive recorder of political or social scenes. There is invariably a sharper edge, where humour tips over into satire and more sympathetic moments of reserve slip into pathos.

© Daniel and Teresa Topolski

Fig. 26 Feliks Topolski
*Self-portrait*, c.1987
Oil on board, 89 × 61 cm
(35¹⁄₁₆ × 24″)

This self-portrait was painted towards the end of the artist's life. Another self-portrait appears in the lower right corner of section 1 of *In the Streets* – the opening sequence of the Coronation frieze (see page 64).

Topolski's arrival in London transformed his life. Apart from extending the range of his art, he also formed a number of influential friendships with writers, artists, intellectuals, and on occasion heads of state. It was Topolski's great fortune to make friends easily with people whatever their background so that his publications, including his autobiography, are an important record of British cultural life over several decades. An early contact in London was with the Irish playwright and critic George Bernard Shaw (1856–1950) with whom Topolski worked closely on theatrical projects and illustrated publications of some of his plays (*Geneva, Pygmalion* and *In Good King Charles's Golden Days*). The collaboration with Shaw culminated in a book of his own, *Portrait of GBS* (1946), and numerous images including a painted full-length portrait. But at the start, Topolski's life centred around the Café Royal where the artists Augustus John and Jacob Epstein, art historian John Rothenstein, journalist Claud Cockburn, composer Constant Lambert, newspaper editor Gerald Barry and actor Michael Redgrave congregated, amongst many others. It was through this talented group that Topolski gained his first commissions in London. He worked primarily as an illustrator, becoming involved with the *News Chronicle* newspaper and the short-lived humorous journal *Night and Day*, edited by Graham Greene and to which Evelyn Waugh, Anthony Powell and John Betjeman also contributed. Topolski adopted the bohemian lifestyle that he encountered on his arrival in London for the

rest of his life, particularly after he established his own studios at Little Venice on the Regent's Canal and then under the arches of the Hungerford Bridge on the South Bank. At both places Topolski held open house, famously in 1952 in honour of Pablo Picasso (1881–1973).

By now Topolski had attracted his own circle of artists, writers, musicians, actors and intellectuals. It is a paradox that for nearly all his working life he depicted the Establishment while at the same time standing apart from it. Symptomatic of this attitude is the fact that his achievements received little official recognition in his lifetime (he was elected RA only in 1988 at the age of 81) and that much of his work is now in America. The paintings and drawings which remain in Britain (at the National Portrait Gallery, Imperial War Museum, Tate Collection and Windsor Castle) are not widely known and are waiting to be rediscovered. Some, like the *Memoir of the Century* mural – a 183 metre (600 feet) long, 61 metre (20 feet) high chronicle of the events and personalities that fashioned the twentieth century – are truly remarkable (figs 30 and 31). This state of affairs reflects not so much the quality of Topolski's art as its nature. He poured scorn on official art, saying that 'The airless studios grow stifling. Kick the door open – the hum of life turns into a roar.'

Topolski's own idiosyncratic viewpoint led to a number of publications in his own name soon after his arrival in Britain. *The London Spectacle* (1935), *Paris Scenes and Secrets* (1939) and *Paris Lost* (publication of which was deferred until 1973) are characteristic not only of Topolski's skill in depicting the essence of the social scene, but also of a type of illustrated work that is very evocative of pre-war Britain. As Europe became engulfed by conflict, it was perfectly logical that Topolski should be appointed an official war artist. He was not simply an observer, but also an active participant, in Italy with the Polish 2nd Corps. Topolski experienced the war on most fronts except the Pacific – the Blitz in London, convoys in the Arctic, the jungle in Burma, and the advance into Germany. He also witnessed the after-math of war, going to the concentration camp at Belsen and attending the Nuremberg trials (1945–6). Many of his drawings were reproduced in popular magazines and journals, but they were also collected to form books – *Britain in Peace and War* (1941; fig. 27) with an introduction by James Laver; *Russia in War* (1942) with an introduction by Sir Stafford Cripps; *Three Continents 1944–45* (1945) with an introduction by Maurice Collis; and *88 Pictures* (1951) with an introduction by Harold Acton. In effect, these volumes amount to publications of the artist's sketchbooks.

Following the Second World War Topolski's art entered a more expansive phase. There was a greater concentration on painting during the second half of his life and he produced memorable images that continued the chronicling of the twentieth century. His murals in particular are distinguished by their large scale, unusual technique, and audacious compositions. Topolski was no doubt mindful of Renaissance

Fig. 27 Feliks Topolski
*Park Crescent, Autumn, 1940*
From *Britain in Peace and War*, 2nd edn, Methuen, London, 1946

The first edition of *Britain in Peace and War* was published in November 1941. Park Crescent is distinguished by its Ionic colonnades designed by John Nash in 1812–22 as part of his urban redevelopment of London based on Regent Street (as a 'royal mile') linking Regent's Park and St James's Park. Park Crescent was rebuilt to Nash's designs after sustaining damage during the Second World War.

frescoes, or of the English revival of the art of fresco for historical purposes during the mid-nineteenth century, but his murals recall contemporary works such as Picasso's *Guernica* (1937). At the invitation of Jawaharlal Nehru, Topolski devised the mural entitled *The East* (1949–50), celebrating the independence of India. This was followed by the *Cavalcade of the Commonwealth*, commissioned in 1951 for the Festival of Britain and mounted under one of the arches of Hungerford Bridge. After the Festival the mural was sent for display in the Victoria Memorial Hall in Singapore, but was eventually returned and parts of it incorporated into *Memoir of the Century*. The whole spectrum of Topolski's art and politics is apparent in two other projects of these years. The murals done in 1952 (since erased) for a new housing estate in Finsbury, a suburb of London, illustrated the history of the city with reference to the local community. By contrast, the *Coronation of Queen Elizabeth II* (1960) was painted specifically for Buckingham Palace (see pages 44–81).

Topolski did not allow his passion for travel and drawing to cool. Many of the places he visited in Africa, Asia, the United States of America, the Caribbean, the Middle East and the Far East were experiencing political change. Instinctively, Topolski was present at the moment of crisis, but it was not so much political tension itself that captivated him as human reactions to it. Such projects increased his reputation and the growing acknowledgement of his skill as a draughts-man was reflected in the number of commissions he now began to receive for portrait drawings. The most famous group of his portraits was undertaken for the series of interviews on BBC television in 1963, *Face to Face* (fig. 28). This overlapped with a commission from the University of Texas at Austin for portraits of twenty living British writers. A more controversial commission, related to the *Face to Face* series, was for portraits of the Labour Party Shadow Cabinet in 1963, originally intended for use in a General Election campaign but in the end, as the artist anticipated, rejected because they were too caricatural. Topolski's skills were also deployed in the capacity of official artist at conferences all over the world (for example, the United Nations Security Council in 1966) and on royal tours (including the royal visit to America in 1957).

The artist's concern for the depiction of changing social mores is most clearly evident in two projects sustained over a number of years. Both are of exceptional interest. *Topolski's Chronicle* first appeared in 1953 (fig. 29) and was published as a broadsheet on a fort-nightly basis until 1979. It is essentially a highly personal pictorial journal of his life and times comprising over 3,000 drawings, many of which were reused in other contexts. In Denvir's words, the *Chronicle* 'exemplifies the constantly productive versatility of his draughts-manship, the universality of his interests, and the exuberant acuity of his vision'. It also bears witness to his 'concept of the artist as a figure concerned more with public than with private life'. As a publishing venture the *Chronicle* was experimental. The artist

Fig. 28 Feliks Topolski
*Dame Edith Sitwell*, signed and
inscribed, 1963
Black chalk, 50 × 42.5 cm (19¹¹⁄₁₆ × 16¾″)
Royal Collection (RCIN 451602)

Topolski portrayed Edith Sitwell,
poet and critic, several times. This
drawing, one of many studies, was
made at the time of Dame Edith's
interview with John Freeman for the
BBC television series *Face to Face*. The
sitter was renowned for her eccentricity,
remarkable appearance and exotic form
of dress. Here she wears her 'bird-king's
hat' and a Solongoi ermine jacket.
There was a subsequent interesting
correspondence between artist and
sitter. A painting based on the studies
is now in Austin in the collection of
the University of Texas (The Harry
Ranson Humanities Research Center,
Iconography Collection).

RIGHT
Fig. 29 Feliks Topolski
Coronation Rehearsal, from *Topolski's Chronicle*, No.1, Vol.1, 1953
45.5 × 29 cm (17¹⁵⁄₁₆ × 11⁷⁄₁₆″)

As an official artist Topolski was granted special access to the
Coronation. He attended the dress rehearsal in Westminster
Abbey, but on Coronation Day itself positioned himself
outside the Abbey. The artist made numerous studies many
of which are in the Royal Library, Windsor Castle. Some of
these were incorporated in the first issue of *Topolski's Chronicle*,
as reproduced here, and subsequently used with others for
the Coronation frieze in Buckingham Palace.

Fig. 31 The artist at work on *Memoir of the Century*, begun in 1975. The mural was installed at Nos 151–2, Hungerford Arches, below the bridge that spans the River Thames.

Fig. 30 Feliks Topolski
*Memoir of the Century*, 1975–89
London, South Bank Centre

*Memoir of the Century* is the artist's masterpiece and is an early example of installation art involving film, sound and other such effects. Topolski's visual account of the history of the twentieth century depicts historical incidents combined with personal anecdote.

described it as a 'glut of notes' or 'promptings (being pinned-down memories) for compositional inventions'. It had a deliberately 'rough-and-ready character' and 'its immediacy and flexible format had to be invented'.

Related to the *Chronicle* is *Memoir of the Century* (1975–89), a mural on a huge scale in a space created under two of the arches of Hungerford Bridge (figs 30 and 31). It is really an installation and significantly it is unfinished, as though emphasising that history will continue after the death of the artist. Indeed, shortly after Topolski's memorial service in the church of St Martin-in-the-Fields in 1989, the Berlin Wall was pulled down – a political transformation that would not have escaped his recording eye. The subject of the *Memoir* is really how the tide of history impacts on the individual. It is a visual diary and the artist continued to be sharply aware of history even at an advanced age. Often he experienced history through the eyes of his children and wide circle of friends, so that he was as much a child of the 1960s, 1970s or 1980s as he had been of the 1930s, 1940s or 1950s. As Topolski himself explains in *Fourteen Letters*:

> The *Memoir* evolves naturally out of accumu-lated and overflowing testimony. Its raw material: experiences understood or enigmatic/on-the-spot drawings/to-and-fro associations/dreams – never documentation of events unwitnessed. It is a painting, not a potted history – thus its chron-ology is skeletal, as it oscillates between images and abstractions of memories. The work is open-ended, in constant progress . . .
>
> The facts of my life, spread over the globe and woven into the history of this century, were pinned down by me in drawing on the spot from very early days. These drawings, masses of them, are the main fodder of this *Memoir*. But the *Memoir*, being a painting, develops its own form, the images and story-telling merging with the unifying movement of colour. . . .
>
> And one more point: I don't work consecu-tively, but move about, returning to add passages and balance abstract against figurative elements. . . . There is no ending. The *Memoir* reaches the present, becomes the Diary and continues from day to day to be cut short only by nature's will.

Topolski is an artist who is difficult to categorise, just as *Fourteen Letters* is no ordinary autobiography. Episodic in style, it combines surrealism with passages written in stream-of-consciousness mode and straight biograph-ical facts together with a creative use of illustrations. Topolski was not an artist who liked to be pigeon-holed and, although precedents can be found for his style and for his proclivity for a certain type of subject-matter, he remained unfettered. Essentially his work in whatever medium – chalk, pencil, brush and ink – was wholly dependent on line. Rhapsodic and agile, his line leaps across the paper like a bird in flight. Often lines are redrawn at speed for this is kinetic art, always energetic, volatile, highly charged, and often explosive. The French painter Eugène Delacroix (1798–1863) believed that an artist should possess the skill to draw a body in the moment between it falling from a window and hitting the ground. Topolski's art had a similar urgency and also a sense of exploration, as the scientist and broadcaster Jacob Bronowski (1908–74) pointed out in *The Ascent of Man* (1973): 'We are aware that Topolski's pictures do not so much fix the face as explore it; that the artist is tracing the detail as if by touch; and that each line that is added strengthens the picture but never makes it final.' Of the artists of today Frank Auerbach (b.1931) may be said to have a similar style in his works on paper.

Topolski's artistic credo was based on the primacy of drawing and the immediacy of the moment. He eschewed the stasis of the studio and preferred to work from life while on the move:

> My drawing 'in terrain' (because my painting is another matter) is of a seismographic inspiration: my hand/eye react instinctively and selectively and knit together the elements which may be gathered while I move/travel through or take part in an action; the page receives and accumulates the visual messages, and if the 'high' of tension and the response of the hand are inexplicably right, the notes (best if in batches) 'come off'. Movement/character, not form, seem their *raison d'être*.

There is a direct link between the evidence gathered in the drawings and the paintings of Topolski, as he himself declared:

> My painting moves, of course, still further into the creative (away from re-creative) process: I never set myself to enlarge and copy a sketch in painting; I paint crowded (over-crowded to those conditioned by castrated one-element aesthetics) IMAGES, fed on the essences squeezed out of numerous drawings – raw material; on memory, fantasies, politics, lurid news . . .'

Topolski acquired a style that served his purposes in depicting the all-inclusive nature of modern subject-matter – 'man's grotesqueries'. It is in fact with those artists most engaged with contemporary life from whatever century that Topolski ultimately has a kinship – Pisanello, Rembrandt, Callot, Delacroix, Daumier, Guys, Ensor, Dix, Rivera, Picasso and Kokoschka. Topolski's reputation undoubtedly suffered from his predilection for the immediate and the ephemeral rather than the universal and he has been too easily dismissed as a mere illustrator or caricaturist. Yet he recognised, as indeed Leonardo da Vinci had before him, that chance or accident are as revealing and compelling as the application of any wider system of knowledge. Topolski claimed – not unexpectedly and by no means irrationally – that his art had a universal appeal conceived on an epic scale. In 1946 he had argued in a Third Programme radio talk for the importance of:

> an art of synthesis – painting fed on reality – the reality of today, which is that of the awareness of multitudes on the move, of global oneness torn by conflicts – and achieved, not by retrogression into 'realism', but through the formal liberty won by modern art. An EPIC art, to match our time . . . This is the right moment to help the new life springing up in visual art. The yielding of the walls of public buildings for mural painting will most certainly draw the artists from their shells, forcing the growth of likely talents up and away from drawing-room canvases. Michelangelo's vision, had it been squashed into the easel pictures of today, would never have expanded into the miracle it is. How unfulfilled he would have been without the Sistine Chapel.

*Memoir of the Century* was Topolski's bid to fulfil this bold ambition, both for himself and to encourage modern artists in Britain.

# Feliks Topolski's
## *Coronation of Queen Elizabeth II*

Although it carried the aura of the Imperial finale, its ceremonials – the forte of this country – were magnificent. Not a sycophant but merely now a breadwinner, this hireling painter drew-painted, and watched the new Old England emerging, re-emerging in a somewhat pauperized imitation of its former self.

From Feliks Topolski, *Fourteen Letters* (1988) on the Coronation of 2 June 1953

The mural by Feliks Topolski commemorating the Coronation of 1953 was commissioned in 1959 by The Duke of Edinburgh. Prince Philip knew the artist and had frequently visited his studio. The details of the commission were quite specific, as the painting was intended for a particular location in Buckingham Palace. This was the Lower Corridor, which extends along the south-west side of the Quadrangle, linking the Ambassadors' Entrance to the Grand Entrance (fig. 32). The prescribed area allowed for a continuous frieze painted on eight boards extending some 19.5 metres (64 feet) along one wall, with a further sequence of six interrupted by five windows on the other. The whole comprises fourteen sections 1.2 metres × 29.0 metres long (3′ 11″ × 95′), divided into two narratives.

On the unbroken wall, the eight sections form a composition entitled *In the Streets*, which shows the various processions on their way to Westminster Abbey (pages 56–71). The six remaining sections on the window wall form a contrasting composition entitled *In the Abbey* that depicts the procession out of Westminster Abbey after the Coronation (pages 72–81). The format of an extended sequence of images was admirably suited to Topolski's talents as a narrative painter.

Almost prophetically, Topolski had acquired the windows of his studio from the annexe that had been specially built for the Coronation at the west door of Westminster Abbey (fig. 33). The annexe, protected on the outside by the set of The Queen's Beasts carved by James Woodford, had been the focal point for the arrivals and departures from the Abbey. It was also the point at which the processions formed up and were dispersed. In 1953 Topolski's studio, under an arch of Hungerford Bridge, was still open to the elements and the glass from the annexe, which he obtained through the Minister of Works, David Eccles, enabled him to enclose the space. It still serves this purpose today (fig. 34).

The frieze is based on the artist's personal impressions of the Coronation (fig. 35). As one of the official artists for the event in 1953, Topolski chose to attend the final rehearsal inside Westminster Abbey (when there was a stand-in for The Queen) and on Coronation Day itself he positioned himself in the streets outside the Abbey. The work took him about one year and it is replete with autobiographical references. There is a self-portrait indicating his own presence on Coronation Day and his son also appears since Daniel Topolski was then at Westminster School,

Fig. 32  Feliks Topolski
*Coronation of Queen Elizabeth II, 2 June 1953* in the Lower
Corridor at Buckingham Palace, 1960

Topolski specially designed his depiction of the
Coronation to fill the walls of the Lower Corridor
on the south-west side of the Quadrangle at
Buckingham Palace. This space had previously
been filled by *The Coronation Procession of William IV*
by R.B. Davis (fig. 36).

© Marcus Harrison

whose pupils traditionally participate in the coronation service. What the painter witnessed was recorded
in numerous drawings that in themselves provided
a vivid depiction of the day. Some of these drawings
appeared in the first issue of *Topolski's Chronicle*, which
began publication in 1953 (see fig. 29 and page 38). The basis
of the frieze, therefore, was numerous drawings made
from the life, as well as the artist's own recollections of
the day. As Topolski said:

> these panoramas are not meant to be a diligent
> document of processional order, uniforms – robes
> and likenesses. It was in agreement with my
> patron that all these should be subjected to the
> compositional sweep, the calligraphy of move-
> ment – to the 'mood' of my interpretation; that
> they should not be information-bound, but be
> 'contemporary paintings', independent of dead-
> wood conventions . . .

It is notable in this context that the sequence *In the
Streets* depicts a cross-section of society – those
officially involved with the processions (including
the road-sweepers) and the crowds merely watching.

Topolski was aware of having to paint for a restricted space and this influenced both the numbers
of figures and their scale. Nonetheless, he achieved his
aim, which was:

> a flow, united-in-discord. But it is all meant
> to be seen in two ways (always in progressing
> survey) – as movement in colour and large
> forms; and in close 'reading' of details . . . The
> gallery is narrow – the paintings deliberately
> demand that the onlooker moves along – they
> are panoramic/ processional and the conven-
> tional stepping back to take the whole in does
> not apply.

Fig. 33 *The Royal Drive begins*
From *Country Life Picture Book of the Coronation*,
2 June 1953, No.46

The most distinctive installation for the Coronation
was the annexe at the west end of Westminster Abbey
guarded by The Queen's Beasts designed by James
Woodford. This annexe provided the necessary space
in which the processions in the Abbey formed up and
dispersed unseen by the crowds.

Fig. 34 Feliks Topolski's studio under Hungerford
Bridge in 1953, from *Fourteen Letters, An Autobiography*,
(London, Faber and Faber, 1988)

The artist occupied this studio at No.158 Hungerford
Arches from 1953. For protection from the elements
he acquired the glass from the annexe made for the
Coronation at Westminster Abbey the previous year
(see left).

Fig. 35 Feliks Topolski planning the *Coronation of Queen Elizabeth II, 2 June 1953* in his studio in 1960

The artist drew a series of preparatory sketches in watercolour before embarking on painting the Coronation frieze. For this purpose he referred back to the studies he had made in 1953, some of which he had published as part of *Topolski's Chronicle* (fig. 29).

Fig. 36 Richard Barrett Davis (1782–1854)
*The Coronation Procession of William IV, 8 September 1831* (detail)
Oil on canvas, 71.1 × 3913 cm (28″ × 128′5″)
Royal Collection (RCIN 405989–405998)

Davis was Animal Painter to both George IV and William IV. His *Coronation Procession of William IV* is painted in ten sections of which this is the climax, showing the Gold State Coach with the King and Queen Adelaide on their way to Westminster Abbey. Quite apart from sharing the same position in the Lower Corridor in Buckingham Palace, the painting by Davis provided Topolski with a prototype for his own composition with its emphasis on the processional.

Topolski's Coronation frieze replaced a similar panoramic work in the Lower Corridor of Buckingham Palace, *The Coronation Procession of William IV* (1831) by Richard Barrett Davis which now hangs in the Main Carriage House in the Royal Mews (fig. 36). This is a very literal record of the procession from Constitution Hill to Westminster Abbey and its dependence on silhouetted forms reduces its visual impact. Various other painted depictions of earlier coronations had been produced intermittently. George Jones had chosen to depict the coronation banquet of George IV in Westminster Hall (see fig. 10). By contrast, a host of artists was on hand to record the coronation of Queen Victoria – Sir George Hayter (fig. 37), C. R. Leslie and John Martin – each of whom chose a different moment in the ceremony. For subsequent coronations, artists seem almost to have adopted a formula. This can be seen in works by Edwin Austin Abbey (fig. 38) and Laurits Tuxen for King Edward VII; John Bacon, Louis Gillot and Frank Owen Salisbury for King George V; and Salisbury again for King George VI (fig. 39). All are static, formal, unified compositions, and it was not until Sir Terence Cuneo's painting *The Coronation of Queen Elizabeth II*, with its higher, more dramatic viewpoint (clearly influenced by the artist's position in Westminster Abbey but also by cinematic techniques) that a less conventional image was produced (figs 40 and 41). All of these twentieth-century paintings illustrate one moment in the coronation service – in Cuneo's case it is The Duke of Edinburgh paying homage. In Topolski's frieze there is no reference to any part of the service or even to the Crowning itself.

Beyond the example set by R. B. Davis in his depiction of William IV's coronation procession, the commission may have encouraged Topolski to follow other precedents. In writing about the frieze he himself refers to the north Italian painter Andrea Mantegna (c.1431–1506) and in the context of the Royal Collection he could only have had in mind the *Triumphs of Caesar* in the Lower Orangery at Hampton Court Palace. The nine canvases comprising the *Triumphs* were painted in Mantua for Francesco Gonzaga II, ruler of that city, over a ten-year period (c.1485–94) and were acquired by Charles I in 1629 (fig. 42). Mantegna's triumphal procession, based on classical sources, extends along nine canvases that were originally divided by pilasters, which heightens the illusion of a passing procession. The *Triumphs* are, however, on a huge scale and it is likely that a more direct influence on Topolski were the narrative panels decorating the

Fig. 37  Sir George Hayter (1792–1871)
*The Coronation of Queen Victoria, 28 June 1838,*
signed and dated 1839
Oil on canvas, 255.3 × 381 cm (100½ × 150″)
Royal Collection (RCIN 405409)

Hayter was Principal Painter in Ordinary to Queen Victoria and painted her State Portrait in 1838, as well as ceremonial pictures commemorating events at the beginning of the reign. The artist was in Westminster Abbey during the coronation and depicted the moment just after the Crowning. The view of the Queen in profile emphasises her youthfulness and her stillness is contrasted with the clamour around her. This large picture took two years to paint. Members of Queen Victoria's family can be seen in the royal box in the background.

Fig. 38  Edwin Austin Abbey (1852–1911)
*The Coronation of King Edward VII, 9 August 1902*, 1902–7
Oil on canvas, 272 × 455.4 cm (107¹⁄₁₆ × 179¼″)
Royal Collection (RCIN 404612)

Edwin Austin Abbey was born in Philadelphia and
initially gained a reputation as an illustrator before
becoming a history painter. He came to London c.1880.
His depiction of the coronation of King Edward VII is on
a massive scale and shows the moment of Crowning
by the Archbishop of Canterbury, the aged Frederick
Temple. The artist observed the ceremony from a similar
position to Hayter (fig. 37), but adopts a slightly different
viewpoint. In the background is the royal box before
which stands Queen Alexandra. The coronation was
due to be held in June, but had to be postponed until
August while the King recovered from a sudden attack
of peritonitis.

Fig. 39 Frank Owen Salisbury (1874–1962)
*The Coronation of King George VI, 12 May 1937*, signed and dated 1938
Oil on canvas, 260.5 × 459.9 cm (102½ × 181 1/16″)
Royal Collection (RCIN 407573), on loan to the Palace
of Westminster

Salisbury was one of the leading portrait painters of his day
and was much in demand in the first half of the twentieth
century, painting many fine ceremonial pictures during the
reign of King George V. Salisbury's depiction of the coronation
of King George VI is on a comparable scale with Abbey's painting
of that of King Edward VII. Compositionally, it is an
exercise in verticals and horizontals with a subtle use of
light. Like Hayter and Abbey, the details of the painting
were discussed with the sovereign. Salisbury's view is
traditional and shows the royal box in which both Queen
Mary and the young Princess Elizabeth are visible with
Queen Elizabeth seated below. The artist made a model of
the scene and painted much of the picture in Westminster
Abbey itself. The finished picture was shown first at the
Royal Academy in London, then at the World's Fair in
New York, and afterwards in Australia and New Zealand.

Fig. 40 Sir Terence Cuneo (1907–96)
*The Coronation of Queen Elizabeth II, 2 June 1953,*
signed and dated 1954
Oil on canvas, 213.8 × 305.4 cm (84⅛ × 120¼″)
Royal Collection (RCIN 404470)

Fig. 41 Sir Terence Cuneo (1907–96)
Study for *The Coronation of Queen Elizabeth II,
2 June 1953*, 1953
Oil on canvas, 76.5 × 63.5 cm (30⅛ × 25″)
Royal Collection (RCIN 101000)

Fig. 42 Andrea Mantegna (c.1430/31–1506)
*The Triumphs of Caesar*, c.1485–94
Tempera on canvas, 270.4 × 2526.3 cm (106½″ × 82′ 9″)
Royal Collection (RCIN 403958–403966)

*The Triumphs of Caesar* has been displayed at Hampton Court
Palace since the seventeenth century and is one of the
most extensive and famous works of Italian Renaissance
art in Britain. Mantegna's composition is one continuous
procession spread over nine canvases and might have been
of interest to Topolski.

Fig. 43  Francesco Pesellino (c.1422–57)
*The Triumph of David*, c.1440–50
Tempera on panel, 43.2 × 177.8 cm (17 × 70″)
London, National Gallery  (NG 6580)

The narrative scenes on marriage chests are on
a reduced scale with the processions placed in
a panoramic setting, but the horizontal thrust
of the composition would have been of interest
to Topolski.

Fig. 44  Rembrandt van Rijn (1606–69)
*Belshazzar's Feast*, signed and dated 163?, c.1636–8
Oil on canvas, 167.6 × 209.2 cm (66 × 82⅓″)
London, National Gallery  (NG 6350)

Rembrandt's broad chiaroscural style and the
dramatic effect created by silhouetting figures
was undoubtedly well known to Topolski.
Contorted poses and exaggerated gestures
are also significant stylistic features shared by
both artists.

gilt wooden chests (*cassoni*) which were a feature of the early Italian Renaissance, particularly in the context of marriage (fig. 43). The subject-matter of these panels was often based on classical or biblical history and sometimes Italian vernacular literature, but it is the treatment of the narrative that is of interest for Topolski's Coronation frieze. The scenes either flow in one direction along the panels or else comprise separate incidents creating a pattern of movement across the surface. Topolski combines both narrative devices so that the figures move parallel to the picture plane and also towards the viewer or else into depth. The dynamism is not just linear: it is also derived from the artist's treatment of the space. Another telling feature is the chiaroscuro effect achieved by using dark paint against the prepared white ground of the support, relieved only in parts by accents of colour used in a restricted way for descriptive purposes. The

use of chiaroscuro is reminiscent of the way in which Rembrandt employed it so dramatically in paintings such as *Belshazzar's Feast* (c.1636–8; fig. 44) and *The Conspiracy of the Batavians* (1661), or in many of his prints.

Topolski's Coronation frieze is an unusual work in its scale, format, size and ambition. The artist set out to recreate an outburst of national emotion and in doing this he combined the overall effect of a momentous occasion with a sense of the particular. It is this interaction that absorbs the viewer's attention. The excitement that is the hallmark of the brushstrokes is also found in the artist's own prose description of the Coronation:

Subdued pent-up graces of 'before-the-war', only tentatively picking up the threads – and suddenly this burst into a glamorous allegory – real enough, yet more: sharper in focus and

colour, fuller in emotion, since staged against the changed, greyer normality.

This parade (bracketed by the populace) gathered round the pivot of English hierarchy the utmost of the period's harmonies and contradictions, established prides and aspirations, the West and the East, the Left and the Right, the Two – and the Third World, and sent it all in a moving frieze (personified and haute-coutured for their roles of the manifest masters and the masterful) to pass in selective metaphors in front of me (as if solely for my wishful-filment) – the grand curtain-taking by protagonists of the multi-spectacle I had to circle the globe to watch in sequences. A miraculous gratuity.

The Coronation brought my old themes to a marvellous climax.

*"Phew!"*

Figs 45–59  Feliks Topolski
*Coronation of Queen Elizabeth II, 2 June 1953*, signed and dated 1960
Sections 1–8 *In the Streets*
Sections 9–14 *In the Abbey*
Oil on board, sections 1–8 each 122 × 243 cm (48$^{1}/_{16}$ × 95$^{5}/_{8}$″),
sections 9–14 each 123 × 160 cm (48$^{3}/_{8}$ × 63″)
Royal Collection (RCIN 405225–405238)

4                                                                                                                3

*In the Streets,* sections 4–1

(Topolski designed *In the Streets* to be viewed as it would be
when walking through the Lower Corridor in Buckingham
Palace. To be viewed 'chronologically', therefore, it should
be read from right to left.)

OVERLEAF
*In the Streets*, section 2 (detail)

*In the Streets*, sections 5–8

OVERLEAF
*In the Streets*, section 7 (detail)

*In the Streets*, section 1

1 The coach of the Speaker of the
   House of Commons
2 The Lord Mayor of London's procession
3 People asleep on pavements the night before
4 Peers and peeresses on their way to
   Westminster Abbey
5 The Earl Marshal (The Duke of Norfolk)
6 The Lord High Chancellor
   (The Lord Simonds)
7 Feliks Topolski

*In the Streets,* section 2

1 Carriage procession of Colonial rulers with
   mounted escort
2 The Right Hon. Sir Winston Churchill
3 HM Queen Salote of Tonga
4 Royal and other representatives of
   foreign states

*In the Streets*, section 3

1 Carriage procession of HM Queen Elizabeth
  The Queen Mother with HRH Princess Margaret
2 Carriage procession of their Royal Highnesses
  The Princes and Princesses of the Blood Royal

*In the Streets*, section 4

1  Press photographers
2  The Queen's procession opens with
   the massed bands of foot guards
3  St John Ambulance Brigade
4  Street cleaners
5  Viewers in stands

*In the Streets,* section 5

1 The 'Dissenters':
a Julian Huxley
b Bertrand Russell
c Augustus John
d Aneurin Bevan
2 The Colonial, Commonwealth and United
Kingdom Contingent and Chiefs of Staff
3 Pipers of the Regular Scottish Regiments
and of the Brigade of Gurkhas

*In the Streets*, section 6

1 Air escort of Delta bombers
2 The public
3 The Queen's Bargemaster and
  twelve Watermen
4 The Yeomen of the Guard
5 The Queen's Escort of Officers from the Colonial
  and Commonwealth Contingents

*In the Streets*, section 7

1   The Gold State Coach conveying HM The Queen
    and HRH The Duke of Edinburgh

*In the Streets*, section 8

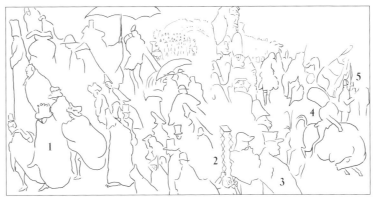

1 Peers, official guests and public disperse
   after the ceremony
2 Spectators using 'periscopes' to watch
   the procession
3 Chelsea pensioner
4 Equerries and Aides-de-Camp to The Queen
5 The Sovereign's Standard

*In the Abbey*, sections 9–14

(It was the artist's intention that *In the Abbey* could be viewed from left to right or right to left. As hung in the Lower Corridor in Buckingham Palace each panel can also be seen as a separate composition.)

12              13              14

*In the Abbey*, section 9

1 Members of the Royal Family:
  a HM Queen Elizabeth The Queen Mother
  b HRH Princess Margaret
  c HRH Prince William of Gloucester
2 Choirboys
3 The Dean of Westminster (The Very Reverend
  Alan Campbell Don)
4 The Cross of Westminster borne by The Reverend
  C. Hildyard
5 Officers of Arms

PREVIOUS PAGE
*In the Abbey*, section 12 (detail)

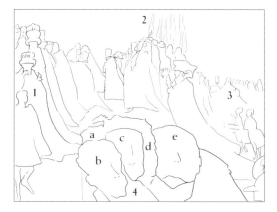

*In the Abbey,* section 10

1   Officers of the Orders of Knighthood
2   The Standards
3   The Keeper of the Jewel House
4   Prime Ministers:
   a   Doctor The Hon. D. F. Malan (Union of South Africa)
   b   The Hon. Jawaharlal Nehru (India)
   c   The Hon. D. Senanayalce (Ceylon)
   d   The Right Hon. R. G. Menzies (Australia)
   e   The Right Hon. Sir Winston Churchill
     (the United Kingdom)

*In the Abbey*, section II

1   The Archbishop of York (The Most Reverend
    Cyril Forster Garbett)
2   The Lord High Chancellor (The Lord Simonds)
3   The Archbishop of Canterbury (The Most Reverend
    Geoffrey Francis Fisher)
4   HRH The Duke of Edinburgh
5   The Gentlemen-at-Arms
6   Foreign and colonial rulers or their representatives

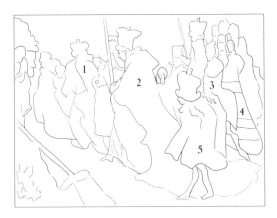

*In the Abbey,* section 12

1 Peers carrying the Regalia
2 The Sword of State borne by the Marquess of Salisbury
3 The Gentleman Usher of the Black Rod
  (Lieutenant-General Sir Brian Horrocks)
4 The Right Hon. The Lord Mayor of London
  (Sir Rupert De la Bère)
5 Garter Principal King of Arms
  (The Hon. Sir George Bellew)

*In the Abbey*, section 13

1 HM The Queen
2 The Bishop of Durham (The Right Reverend
  Arthur Michael Ramsay)
3 The Bishop of Bath and Wells (The Right Reverend
  Harold William Bradfield)
4 The Maids-of-Honour:
  a Lady Jane Vane-Tempest-Stewart
  b Lady Anne Coke
  c Lady Moyra Hamilton
  d Lady Mary Baillie-Hamilton
  e Lady Jane Heathcote-Drummond-Willoughby
  f Lady Rosemary Spencer-Churchill
5 The Mistress of the Robes (The Dowager Duchess
  of Devonshire)
6 The Gentlemen-at-Arms

*In the Abbey*, section 14

1  Silver Stick-in-Waiting
2  Equerries
3  Gold Stick-in-Waiting
4  The Keeper of Her Majesty's Privy Purse
5  Pages of Honour
6  The Yeomen of the Guard

# The Coronation Dress and Robes

HUGH ROBERTS

SINCE THE NORMAN CONQUEST there have only been five queens regnant of England and later Great Britain: Mary I and Elizabeth I in the sixteenth century, Queen Anne in the eighteenth century, Queen Victoria in the nineteenth century and Queen Elizabeth II in the twentieth and twenty-first. While the principal features of the coronation service and the ceremonial attached to it have evolved without any particular regard to the sex of the sovereign, certain aspects, particularly dress, have inevitably come to carry more weight for a queen regnant than for a king. Among the most significant concerns for a female sovereign, shared to some extent with a queen consort, is the form and decoration of the dress to be worn for her arrival at Westminster Abbey before the coronation and on leaving the Abbey afterwards. Tradition simply dictates that sovereigns should arrive wearing Parliament Robes of crimson or scarlet velvet trimmed with ermine and leave wearing purple velvet Robes of Estate. By contrast, the ritual vestments donned by the sovereign (whether male or female) for the actual ceremony are very carefully prescribed; and the design of these (most of which are still in use for coronations) has remained broadly unchanged since the time of Charles II.

For both queens regnant and consort, the day of the coronation has almost always been the occasion for the conspicuous display of rich dress. In the coronation portrait of the first Queen Elizabeth, for example (fig. 60), that monarch is depicted wearing a richly embroidered and jewel-encrusted silver and gold dress with tightly fitting bodice and full skirt in the court fashion of the day. The elderly and gouty Queen Anne wore beneath her crimson velvet robe a dress of gold tissue richly embroidered with jewels, although little of this was seen since she was carried into the Abbey in a chair. Equally little was seen on her departure, swathed in a purple velvet robe: the latter seems to have been formed more like a cloak than the modern robe with its shoulder fastening and long train. Queen Victoria eschewed an elaborate dress (fig. 61): she wore a crimson velvet and white satin surcoat beneath her Parliament Robe and, it seems, a very simple underdress beneath. In design, the surcoat followed contemporary fashion, consisting of a close-fitting bodice and undersleeves trimmed with white and gold laces and a full skirt of white satin. However, most of this was concealed by the robe, of which it forms an integral part; and neither during the ceremony itself, when the traditional vestments played the dominant part, nor in pictorial records of the event does this costume, still less the underdress, make any significant impact or give any indication of the way in which coronation dresses and robes were to develop in the twentieth century.

It is to the dress – and particularly the robe – worn by Queen Alexandra for the coronation of King Edward VII in 1902 that we must look to see the ancestry of Queen Elizabeth II's Coronation Dress and Robe (fig. 62). For her dress, Queen Alexandra

Fig. 60  Anon
*Elizabeth I in Coronation Robes*, c.1600–10 after an earlier
portrait of 1558
Oil on panel, 127.3 × 99.7 cm (50⅛ × 39¼″)
London, National Portrait Gallery (5175)

The hieratic pose underlines the importance of this
early coronation portrait of Elizabeth I. As an image the
likeness was also used on seals, coins and documents
for the transaction of the business of government.

Fig. 61  Sir George Hayter (1792–1871)
*Queen Victoria in Coronation Robes*, signed and dated 1840
Oil on canvas, 270.7 × 185.8 cm (106½ × 73⅛″)
Royal Collection (RCIN 405185)

This is a life-size replica of the artist's State Portrait for
which he had made studies in Westminster Abbey. Here,
however, there is little hint of architecture and more
emphasis on the 'Homage Chair' in which Queen Victoria
is seated beneath an elaborate canopy. Hayter uses aspects
of religious iconography – the upward glance and the
direction of light – to increase the impact of the portrait.

Fig. 62 Sir Luke Fildes (1843–1927)
*Queen Alexandra in Coronation Robes*, signed and dated 1905
Oil on canvas, 265.3 × 170.6 cm (104⁷⁄₁₆ × 67⅛″)
Royal Collection (RCIN 404554)

The coronation dress designed for Queen Alexandra was particularly elaborate and reflected her sense of style and love of jewellery. Little attention was paid to precedent: 'I know better than all the milliners, and antiquaries, I shall wear exactly what I like – and so shall all my ladies – *Basta!*' Fildes, who achieved success earlier in his career by painting subjects of social realism, has painted the full-length portrait on a grand scale, emphasising the height of the figure and the intricacy of the coronation dress.

Fig. 63 Sir William Samuel Henry Llewellyn (1863–1941)
*Queen Mary in Coronation Robes*, signed and dated 1911–12
Oil on canvas, 279.9 × 183.7 cm (110³⁄₁₆ × 72⁵⁄₁₆″)
Royal Collection (RCIN 402024)

While Sir Luke Fildes painted the State Portrait of King George V, Queen Mary's was undertaken by Sir William Llewellyn who later became President of the Royal Academy. He began work in 1911, but sittings were interrupted by the State Visit to India (November 1911–February 1912) culminating in the Delhi Durbar. Work continued on the portrait in 1912 when it was shown at the Royal Academy.

chose an elaborate form of contemporary court design, but with a slightly medieval flavour imparted by the upstanding wired collar. The dress, which was made in Paris by Thorin-Blossier, was of gold tissue and white net embroidered with gold spangles and gold and silver floral sprays. The latter included Indian flora and the National Emblems of rose and thistle (the latter not easy to distinguish). The robe (of purple velvet for a queen consort, but of a shade specially selected by Queen Alexandra) was elaborately embroidered by Princess Louise's Ladies' Work Society with emblems of the British Empire including the National Emblems (rose, shamrock, thistle), Saxon crowns, fleurs-de-lis, the Star of India and the Royal Crown, the last two not strictly appropriate for a queen consort. King Edward's robes by contrast were quite plain.

The design of Queen Mary's purple robe for the coronation of King George V, which was also embroidered by the Ladies' Work Society, used much the same vocabulary of ornament, including the National and Imperial Emblems, but with the addition of the Queen's initial M (fig. 63). The purple velvet was woven by Warner's of Braintree in Essex. Queen Mary's coronation dress, of cream satin, was made in London by Reville & Rossiter and incorporates an elaborate embroidered scheme of the National Emblems, waves representing the oceans connecting the different parts of the Empire, and the lotus and Star of India. For the coronation of 1937, Queen Elizabeth's robe, embroidered

Fig. 64  Sir Gerald Kelly (1879–1972)
*Queen Elizabeth in Coronation Robes*, 1938–45
Oil on canvas, 276 × 184.7 cm (108⅝ × 72¹¹⁄₁₆″)
Royal Collection (RCIN 403423)

Kelly painted the State Portraits of King George VI and
Queen Elizabeth at Windsor Castle during the Second
World War. He made numerous preparatory oil-sketches
and, for the background, asked Sir Edwin Lutyens to
make models in the style of the Viceroy's House at Delhi.
Like the state portraits painted for the two previous
reigns, these are on a large scale with an emphasis on
the monumentality of the figures and a rigorous system
of perspective. Kelly was described as 'the most reliable
portrait painter of his time'. He later became President
of the Royal Academy.

by the Royal School of Needlework, developed an even more elaborate iconographic scheme (fig. 64). This included the rose, thistle, leek and shamrock for Great Britain, lotus for India, protea for South Africa, maple for Canada, fern for New Zealand and mimosa or wattle for Australia, together with two interlaced E's. The National and Imperial Emblems were also included in the embroidery of Queen Elizabeth's cross-cut ivory satin coronation dress, executed in gold thread, diamanté and spangles and made by Handley Seymour of New Bond Street.

It is a short step from these designs of 1937 to the Robe of Estate and Coronation Dress made for The Queen in 1953 (figs 65–74). The purple velvet for the Robe was woven in two lengths of 20 yards (18.3 metres), each 21 inches (53 cm) wide, by Warner & Sons using silk from Lady Hart Dyke's silk farm at Lullingstone, Kent. The silk for Queen Elizabeth's robe in 1937 had come from the same source. The Robe is of simpler design overall than Queen Elizabeth's, comprising a border of wheat ears and olive branches symbolising peace and plenty, centred at the bottom of the train by The Queen's crowned cypher. As in 1937, the embroidery was designed and carried out by the Royal School of Needlework. The embroideresses worked a total of 3,500 hours between March and May 1953 and the Robe was made up by Ede and Ravenscroft of Chancery Lane. The Queen chose not to wear a surcoat with either the Parliament Robe or Robe of Estate, thereby giving additional prominence to the Coronation Dress itself.

The Coronation Dress, which is made of white satin and elaborately embroidered, was designed by the royal couturier Mr (later Sir) Norman Hartnell, who had begun making clothes for Queen Mary, subsequently worked for Queen Elizabeth, and until his death in 1979 was The Queen's principal dressmaker. It has a fitted bodice with short sleeves, square-cut neckline and full, flaring skirt, slightly trained. The design of the embroidery, executed in seed pearls, crystals, coloured silks and gold and silver thread, was particularly carefully thought out to take account of the changes that had occurred since 1937 in the composition of the Empire and the evolution of the Commonwealth. On the skirt, the embroidery is laid out in three 'tiers' of overlapping panels framed by ribbed embroidered bands of gold crystals against a lattice-work design, and with a broad undulating lower border. The National Emblems appear as follows: the Tudor rose (for England) on the short sleeves, the leek in flower (for Wales) on the first tier of the skirt, the shamrock (for Ireland) on the second and the thistle (for Scotland) on the third. The lower border of the skirt includes every emblem of the Commonwealth surrounding the Tudor rose. The Commonwealth Emblems (similar to those chosen for Queen Elizabeth's robe in 1937) are maple leaf (Canada), wattle flower (Australia), fern (New Zealand), protea (South Africa), lotus (India), another lotus (Ceylon, now Sri Lanka) and wheat, cotton and jute (Pakistan).

Hartnell's original design (fig. 65) was carried out almost to the letter, the only slight changes being in the shaping of the sleeves and the omission of embroidery on the front of the bodice. The dress was made in the workroom at 26 Bruton Street under the supervision of Hartnell's 'first hand', Madame Isabelle, and Hartnell himself added an additional shamrock on the left side of the skirt for good luck. With The Queen's permission, Hartnell's sketches were first shown to the press at Bruton Street on 1 June 1953, the day before the Coronation.

Fig. 65 Sir Norman Hartnell (1901–79)
*Queen Elizabeth II in Coronation Robes*, 1953
Watercolour and bodycolour over pencil, 51.5 × 38.5 cm
(20¼ × 15³⁄₁₆″)
Royal Collection (RCIN 451858)

Norman Hartnell was the first couturier to be knighted
when he received that honour at the time of the Silver
Jubilee in 1977. He served for many years as couturier
to senior members of the Royal Family and made
both the wedding dress and the Coronation Dress of
Queen Elizabeth II. Considerable excitement was
generated at the time concerning the designs of these
dresses which are characteristic of Hartnell's fulsome
style, using extensive embroidery, pearls and other
lustrous forms of decoration.

Fig. 66  Sir Herbert James Gunn (1893–1964)
*Queen Elizabeth II in Coronation Robes*, 1953–4
Oil on canvas, 244.5 × 152.9 cm (96¼ × 60³⁄₁₆″)
Royal Collection (RCIN 404386)

Figs 67 and 68 The Coronation Dress and Robe of Estate of Queen Elizabeth II, 1953. The Dress was designed by Norman Hartnell and incorporates National and Commonwealth emblems. The Robe was embroidered by the Royal School of Needlework.

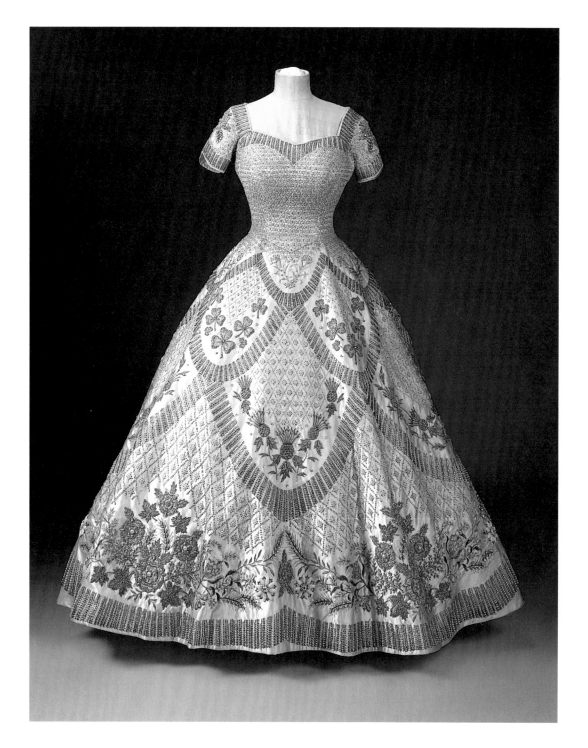

Fig. 69 Detail of the embroidered shamrocks, representing Ireland, and flowering leeks, representing Wales.

Fig. 70 Detail of the embroidered thistles, representing Scotland.

LEFT Fig. 71 The Coronation Dress of Queen Elizabeth II, 1953, front view.

Fig. 72  The Coronation Dress of Queen Elizabeth II, 1953, three-quarter view.

Fig. 73  The Coronation Dress of Queen Elizabeth II, 1953, back view.

Fig. 75 Anna Zinkeisen (1901–76)
*The Coronation Bouquet*, signed and dated 1953
Oil on canvas, 63.9 × 76.5 cm (25³/₁₆ × 30⅛″)
Royal Collection (RCIN 407248)

OPPOSITE
Fig. 74 Detail of the lower border embroidered with emblems of
the Commonwealth surrounding the Tudor Rose of England.

# Constance Spry's original recipe for Coronation Chicken

## Coronation Chicken (cold) (for 6–8)

2 young roasting chickens
water and a little wine to cover
carrot
a bouquet garni
salt
3–4 peppercorns
cream of curry sauce (*see below*)

Poach the chickens, with carrot, bouquet garni, salt and peppercorns, in water and a little wine, enough barely to cover, for about 40 minutes or until tender. Allow to cool in the liquid. Joint the birds, remove the bones with care. Prepare the sauce given below. Mix the chicken and the sauce together, arrange on a dish, coat with the extra sauce.

For convenience in serving on the occasion mentioned, the chicken was arranged at one end of an oblong dish, and a rice salad as given below was arranged at the other.

## Rice salad

The rice salad which accompanied the chicken was of carefully cooked rice, cooked peas, diced raw cucumber, and finely chopped mixed herbs, all mixed in a well-seasoned French dressing.

## Cream of curry sauce

1 tablespoon oil
2 oz onion, finely chopped
1 dessertspoon curry powder
1 good teaspoon tomato purée
1 wineglass red wine
¾ wineglass water
a bay-leaf
salt, sugar, a touch of pepper
a slice or two of lemon and
    a squeeze of lemon juice, possibly more
1–2 tablespoons apricot purée
¾ pint mayonnaise
2–3 tablespoons lightly whipped cream
a little extra whipped cream

Heat the oil, add onion, cook gently 3–4 minutes, add curry powder. Cook again 1–2 minutes. Add purée, wine, water and bay-leaf. Bring to boil, add salt, sugar to taste, pepper and the lemon and lemon juice. Simmer with the pan uncovered 5–10 minutes. Strain and cool. Add by degrees to the mayonnaise with the apricot purée to taste. Adjust seasoning, adding a little more lemon juice if necessary. Finish with the whipped cream. Take a small amount of sauce (enough to coat the chicken) and mix with a little extra cream and seasoning.

# Bibliography

*Chips: The Diaries of Sir Henry Channon*, ed. with a new introduction by R.R. James, Phoenix Giant, London, 1996

*The Crown Jewels. The History of the Coronation Regalia in the Jewel House of the Tower of London*, ed. C. Blair, 2 vols, The Stationery Office, London, 1998

*The Diary of John Evelyn*, ed. E.S. de Beer, 6 vols, Clarendon Press, Oxford, 1955

*The Illustrated Journies of Celia Fiennes c.1682–c.1712*, ed. C. Morris, Webb and Bower, London, 1982

*The Royal Encyclopedia*, eds. R. Allison and S. Riddell, Macmillan Press, London, 1991

*Self-Portrait with Friends. The Selected Diaries of Cecil Beaton 1926–1974*, ed. R. Buckle, Weidenfeld and Nicolson, London, 1979

*The Shorter Pepys*, selected and edited by Robert Latham, Penguin Books, London, 1987

*The Yale Edition of Horace Walpole's Correspondence*, ed. W.S. Lewis, 48 vols, London, Oxford University Press and New Haven, Yale University Press, 1937–83

I. Bradley, *God Save The Queen. The Spiritual Dimension of Monarchy*, Darton Longman Todd, London, 2002

D. Cannadine, 'The Content, Performance and Meaning of Ritual: The British Monarchy and the "Invention of Tradition", c.1820–1977', in *The Invention of Tradition*, eds. E. Hobsbawm and T. Ranger, Cambridge and New York, Cambridge University Press, 1983, pp. 101–64

H. Carpenter, *Benjamin Britten. A Biography*, Faber and Faber, London, 1993

B. Denvir, P. Ford and F. Topolski, *Topolski's Buckingham Palace Panoramas*, with a foreword by HRH The Prince Philip, Duke of Edinburgh, Quartet Books, London, 1977

B. Denvir, *'Feliks Topolski: Chronicler Extraordinary'*, n.d.

Z. Halls, *Coronation Costume and Accessories, 1685–1953*, The Stationery Office, London, 1973

B. Pimlott, *The Queen. Elizabeth II and the Monarchy*, Golden Jubilee Edition, HarperCollins, London, 2001

E. Shils and M. Young, 'The Meaning of the Coronation', *The Sociological Review*, NS, Vol. I, No. 2, University College of North Staffordshire, Keele, 1953, pp. 63–81

F. Topolski, *Fourteen Letters: An Autobiography*, Faber and Faber, London, 1988

# Index

Figures in italics refer to captions